What Are the Issues with
with
Genetic
Technology?

Eve Hartman and Wendy Meshbesher

Raintree

www.raintreepublishers.co.uk
Visit our website to find out
more information about
Raintree books.

To order:
☎ Phone 0845 6044371
▤ Fax +44 (0) 1865 312263
▣ Email myorders@raintreepublishers.co.uk

Customers from outside the UK please telephone +44 1865 312262

Raintree is an imprint of Capstone Global Library Limited,
a company incorporated in England and Wales having its
registered office at 7 Pilgrim Street, London, EC4V 6LB –
Registered company number: 6695582

Edited by Adam Miller, Andrew Farrow, and
  Adrian Vigliano
Designed by Philippa Jenkins
Original illustrations © Capstone Global Library
  Limited 2012
Illustrated by Medi-mation p8, KJA-artists.com p30
Picture research by Mica Brancic
Originated by Capstone Global Library Ltd
Printed and bound in China by CTPS

ISBN 978 1 406 23385 8 (hardback)
15 14 13 12
10 9 8 7 6 5 4 3 2

British Library Cataloguing in Publication Data
Hartman, Eve.
What are the issues with genetic technology?. -- (Sci-hi)
660.6'5-dc22
A full catalogue record for this book is available from the
British Library.

Acknowledgments
The author and publishers are grateful to the following
for permission to reproduce copyright material: Alamy
p. 35 left (© Lana Sundman); Corbis pp. 5 (epa/© Pedro
Armestre), 15 (© John Springer Collection), 22 (epa/©
Jon Hrusa), 29 (© Owen Franken), 31 (© Reuters/
Jeff J Mitchell), 43 (© Tim Pannell); Getty Images pp.
10 (Taxi/Shioguchi), 11 (Bloomberg/Jack Plunkett),
12 (Bloomberg/Daniel Acker), 24 (Flickr/Christian
Senger), 39 (The Image Bank/Tim Kitchen), 20 left
(Close-up of a baby boy); Reuters p. 41 (Heinz-Peter
Bader); Science Photo Library pp. 9 (Edward Kinsman),
13 (US Department Of Energy/Oak Ridge National
Laboratory), 14 (Eye of Science), 38 (Visuals Unlimited/
Margaret Oechsli), 20 right (AJ Photo), 6 bottom (Eye of
Science); Shutterstock pp. 4 (© Vivid Pixels), 7 (© Pavel
Shchegolev), 17 (© Alexander Raths), 18 (© Mikhail
Tchkheidze), 19 (© Marcel Jancovic), 25 (© Dirtfoto), 26
(© Veniamin Kraskov), 27 (© Henk Bentlage), 32 (© Shawn
Hempel), 34 (© Jonathan Feinstein), 37 (© Krasowit),
35 right (© imagelab), 6 top (© Pixshots), Contents
page bottom (© Shawn Hempel), Contents page top
(© Veniamin Kraskov). All background design feature
pictures courtesy of Shutterstock.

Main cover photograph of cloning research reproduced
with permission of Science Photo Library (Mauro
Fermariello); inset cover photograph of a chromosome
reproduced with permission of Shutterstock (© Sashkin).

The publisher would like to thank literary consultant
Nancy Harris and content consultant Ann Fullick for their
assistance in the preparation of this book.

Every effort has been made to contact copyright holders
of material reproduced in this book. Any omissions will
be rectified in subsequent printings if notice is given to
the publisher.

Contents

Why do blue roses cause such controversy?

Find out on page 14!

How can DNA send you to prison, or get you out of prison?

Turn to page 32 to find out!

Some words are shown in bold, **like this**. These words are explained in the glossary. You will find important information and definitions underlined, <u>like this</u>.

GENETIC TECHNOLOGY

Genetic technology could offer choices to parents about their babies.

If you were a parent, would you want to choose features for your baby? Would you choose the colour of the baby's eyes or hair, or choose the gender? Maybe you want the baby to have a budding talent in maths, music, or sport. Scientists are studying how to choose or change the features of plants and animals, including humans. Some of these choices are already possible to make, even for human babies. More choices may be possible soon. But should they be? Scientists and the public have only just begun to discuss this question.

GENES AND SCIENCE

Genes are the units that pass from parents to offspring and that determine **traits**. A trait is a clear feature of an **organism** (living thing). Physical traits include height, skin colour, and possessing a feature such as dimples. Other traits include behaviour patterns such as the mating behaviour of animals or the time of year a flower blooms.

Scientists have been studying genes and traits for over 100 years. However, within the past 20 years, scientists have discovered ways to change and alter genes. They can also transfer them from one organism to another. **Genetic technology**, which is also called genetic engineering, involves changing or using genes in ways that do not occur in nature.

Today, many farm crops have been **genetically modified** to increase their resistance to pests. Genes of **bacteria** (tiny living things) have been modified to produce useful products, such as **insulin**. Insulin is a substance that the body makes to help control blood sugar levels.

CONTROVERSY!

Not everyone agrees that genetic technology is worthwhile. Many opponents are concerned that the technology could produce dangerous or unwanted organisms. Others argue that it brings more damage than benefit, especially to food crops. Many people object to the technology on moral and ethical grounds (issues of right versus wrong).

You will learn more about these controversies as you continue reading this book.

Genetically modifed food crops are especially controversial.

5

WHAT ARE GENES?

Genes explain the similarities among these Siberian husky puppies. They explain the differences, too.

The idea of **genes** was proposed in the 1860s by Gregor Mendel, an Austrian monk. Many years later, improvements to microscopes allowed scientists to identify and locate genes in the **cell**. A cell is the smallest building block of a living thing. Genes are found on **chromosomes**. A chromosome is made of a **molecule** called deoxyribonucleic acid or **DNA**. Each gene is a small section of DNA. Almost every cell contains two sets of chromosomes, one from each parent.

Chromosomes appear as worm-like strands when stained and magnified.

The chromosomes are found in the **nucleus** of the cell. When a cell divides it forms two identical cells. When the cell is getting ready to divide, each chromosome acts as a model for the formation of a new, identical chromosome. Each new cell then gets an identical set of chromosomes containing the same genes.

A human cell has 46 chromosomes. Each chromosome contains between a few hundred and many thousands of genes. They hold a total of between 20,000 and 25,000 genes.

GENES ARE EVERYWHERE!

Scientists have studied the cells of all sorts of **organisms**, from single-celled **bacteria** to whales and elephants. In all of these organisms, genes are organized on chromosomes in much the same way as in the human cell.

In bacteria, the chromosome is circular. It is not stored in a nucleus. But as in all organisms, the chromosome contains the set of genes that the bacterial cell needs to survive.

Chromosome number

Every species has a characteristic number of chromosomes in its cells. Do large, advanced species have more chromosomes per cell than simple species? The chart suggests the answer.

Species	Chromosomes per cell
Corn (Zea mays)	20
Green algae (A.mediterranea)	20
Human (Homo sapiens)	46
Dog (Canis familiaris)	78
Goldfish (Carassius auratus)	94

Genes can affect height, but strength and skills develop only with training.

DNA

DNA is the molecule that makes up genes. Compared to other molecules, a molecule of DNA is huge. Yet how can a molecule of any size control the **traits** of the body? The answer lies in the way the parts of DNA are put together.

DNA contains four different parts called **bases** which pair up neatly. The order of these bases acts as a code for making changes in your body. Different genes result in different traits such as eye colour, height, and the age at which you are likely to have your teenage growth spurt.

DNA also plays a role in cancer and other diseases. Certain genes increase the risk of developing cancer of the breast or ovaries. Scientists are finding more and more diseases that are affected by our genes.

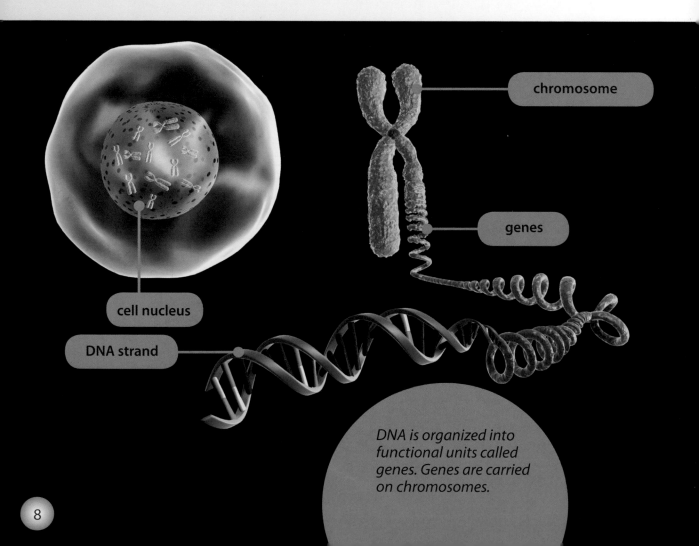

chromosome

genes

cell nucleus

DNA strand

DNA is organized into functional units called genes. Genes are carried on chromosomes.

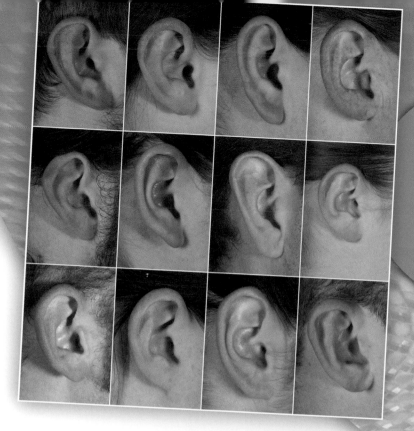

From person to person, subtle differences in DNA affect ear shape and other facial traits.

HUMAN VS. MOUSE

You could easily tell a human and a mouse apart. Humans don't look like trees or dandelions, either. So you might think that these organisms have very different DNA. If so, you would be wrong!

The genetic code is the same for nearly all organisms, as is the process for translating it. As for the DNA itself, many regions of it are identical in plant and animal cells. A human and a mouse have 99 per cent of their DNA in common.

The fact that the DNA of most organisms is very similar makes many kinds of **genetic technology** possible. This is because a gene which works in one organism can often be made to work in another organism. This is the basis of genetic engineering.

Junk DNA

As scientists studied DNA, they were surprised to observe that genes take up only a small fraction of the molecule. Most DNA does not appear to do very much. This part of DNA is called junk DNA. Is junk DNA necessary or important? Scientists continue to ponder and investigate this question.

WHAT GENES CONTROL

Just what traits of the human body do genes control? Genes clearly control eye colour, hair colour, and the shape and size of toes and fingers. Genes also affect height. However, a poor diet or poor general health can affect the height that the body grows to.

Evidence also shows that genes affect personality and intelligence. Talents in maths, music, or art have been observed to run in families, even among children who were separated from their biological parents.

IDENTICAL STRANGERS

Identical twins have exactly the same DNA. By studying twins, scientists can study the extent that genes affect or influence human life.

As infants, identical twins Paula Bernstein and Elyse Schein were adopted by different families. They met for the first time at age 35. They discovered they had similar tastes in music and books, and similar personalities. Yet they also realized they had different values based on their different experiences.

Together the twins wrote *Identical Strangers*, a book about their separation and reunion.

By studying identical twins, scientists hope to learn how genes affect thinking and behaviour.

The Human Genome Project

Between 1990 and 2003, scientists around the world worked to identify every code in human DNA. Scientists are still analyzing the data. They are already using some of the information in practical ways to help them understand and treat genetic diseases. One day they hope to be able to cure them.

One benefit of the Human Genome Project is new technology for sequencing genes. By 2020, a machine might be able to sequence the DNA of an individual human in about 15 minutes! Doctors could use the information to treat patients.

The brown calf is a clone, or genetic duplicate, of its parent (not pictured). You will read more about cloning on page 30.

GENETIC TECHNOLOGY TODAY

Some technologies develop slowly and gradually. This is not the case with **genetic technology**! In the past 20 years, scientists have developed and applied genetic technology that affects people everywhere. Foods, drugs, and medical treatments all come from this technology. As you will discover, though, the technology raises issues about science and **ethics** (the study of right and wrong).

The genes of these corn plants have been altered to help them resist pests.

TRANSGENIC ORGANISMS

In many processes of genetic technology, a useful **gene** is transferred from one **organism** to another. The organisms are often from very different species. Genes from **bacteria** have been transferred to plants and to animals.

Organisms made from transferred genes are called **transgenic organisms**. A transgenic corn plant or sugar beet may look or behave very much like any other plant of its species. But the transferred gene provides a new **trait**, such as resistance to pests.

KNOCKOUTS

Scientists are also using genetic technology to learn how genes operate. One simple way of testing a gene's function is to remove it from the organism. Scientists call the new organism a **knockout**.

As you've already read, mice and humans share about 99 per cent of the same genes. To learn how human genes work, scientists have been studying knockout mice. By comparing the knockout mouse to normal mice, scientists can figure out the gene's function in both mice and humans.

Altering a single gene can cause drastic changes, such as a tripling of body size.

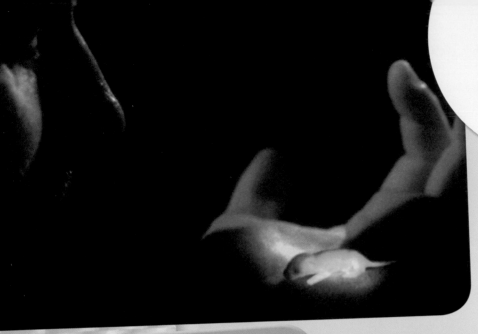

This mouse glows in the dark because of a gene it received from a glowing jellyfish.

Blue roses

By using **conventional methods**, plant scientists and gardeners have bred roses that are red, white, yellow, and shades in between. But a blue colour does not occur naturally in roses, so breeding a blue rose was not possible - until genetic technology arrived.

Scientists have now created blue roses (see the photo on page 26). They have also made other unusual living things, such as a fish that glows in the dark. Some people argue that these products are an improper use of genetic technology. Many people argue against these products on ethical or moral grounds. What do you think?

GENETICALLY MODIFIED CROPS

Today, many of the world's corn and sugar crops are grown from **genetically modified (GM)** plants. These plants were given genes that make them resistant to pests or drought. They are examples of **transgenic plants**, or plants that include genes from other organisms.

One common gene that is now in food crops comes from a type of bacteria. In bacteria, the gene produces a substance that kills young insects that feed on it. The gene now does the same thing in transgenic corn and potatoes, and other crops.

In another chapter you will read much more about GM crops and the controversy surrounding them.

SPIDERS AND MONSTERS?

In a popular movie, the hero is bitten by a GM spider. Soon he can spin webs and climb walls like a spider can. However, this is possible only in fiction. Genetic technology is not likely to create monsters because the genes for such creatures do not exist.

Some seemingly simple **traits**, such as eye colour in humans, depend on many genes that work together in complicated ways. So although an isolated gene can be transferred to a new organism, a large set of genes for a complex trait, such as a head or limb, cannot.

Humans turning into insects or other creatures is a popular theme in science fiction. But it cannot happen in real life, even with genetic technology.

PHARMING

Pharmaceuticals are drugs and medicines. In a practice called **pharming**, scientists use transgenic plants or animals to produce a pharmaceutical. Often the "pharmed" drug is a chemical made normally by the human body.

In one pharming technique, a human gene is transferred to a cow, goat, or other **mammal**. The animal then makes the product of this gene and releases it in its milk. Scientists then collect the product from the milk.

Drugs are made by transgenic bacteria and plants, too. **Insulin** is an example. Insulin is the chemical that helps the body process blood sugar. Human insulin from transgenic organisms can be used to treat **diabetes**. Diabetes is a disease in which the body does not produce enough insulin of its own. When diabetes is not controlled, every organ (body part such as the heart or liver) in the body can be harmed.

Better insulin

Diabetes affects 200 million people worldwide, and the number is growing every year. In the past, insulin for diabetics was expensive and not always of high quality. Pharming can provide effective, low-cost insulin that is chemically identical to human insulin.

RIGHT OR WRONG?

Genetic technology is new, and so are the ethical questions it raises. Is it right to change the genes of plants and animals, even for noble purposes such as improving human health? People are forming different answers to this question. As you read on, try to consider both sides of ethical issues as you form your own opinions about them.

People with diabetes depend on injections of insulin. Genetic technology could provide insulin of high quality and low cost.

FROM PARENTS TO CHILDREN

Scientists have amassed a huge body of knowledge about human **genes**, both from **genetic technology** and other sources. Scientists can now evaluate the genes of babies before they are born. As genetic technology advances, **genetic disorders** (illnesses caused by genes) might disappear from the human population. Other genetic changes are also possible.

A baby's genes can be assessed well before birth. But are genetic assessments worthwhile?

GENETIC COUNSELLING AND TESTS

As we've discussed, genes interact with each other in complicated ways. It is possible that two healthy parents could have a child that suffers from a genetic disorder. The gene for this disorder could be hidden in both parents, then become a problem in the child.

In **genetic counselling**, a geneticist or other expert analyzes the possibility of genetic disorders in a couple's future children. Many couples use genetic counselling to help them decide whether to have children.

A pregnant woman may decide to test the genes of the fetus (developing baby) she is carrying. These tests also help detect genetic disorders that affect whole **chromosomes**, such as Down's syndrome. They also help detect genetic disorders that are linked to the sex of the baby.

Too much information?

People can have their genes tested for many diseases, including Huntington's disease (a loss of nerve function) and Alzheimer's disease (a brain disorder that involves memory loss). Other tests can assess a person's risk of developing certain forms of cancer.

These tests offer both benefits and drawbacks. The results can help patients plan their lives and make important decisions, such as whether to have children. Yet the results can raise fears and anxiety. And what if a patient loses medical insurance because of test results?

Science alone cannot decide whether genetic testing is the right choice. Individuals must choose for themselves.

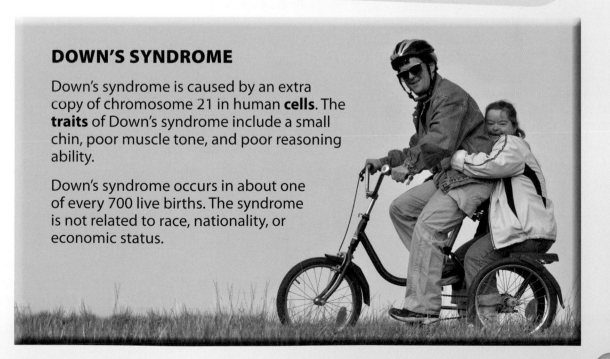

DOWN'S SYNDROME

Down's syndrome is caused by an extra copy of chromosome 21 in human **cells**. The **traits** of Down's syndrome include a small chin, poor muscle tone, and poor reasoning ability.

Down's syndrome occurs in about one of every 700 live births. The syndrome is not related to race, nationality, or economic status.

DESIGNER BABIES?

All over the world, scientists are changing the genes of **bacteria**, plants, and animals such as cows, goats, and mice. But for the most part, changing human genes is illegal. Laws of many nations prevent the creation of a transgenic human baby. Nevertheless, many actions that affect a baby's genetics are legal and common. They are carried out to try and prevent the birth of children affected by serious genetic diseases, which will shorten their lives.

Fertility is the ability to conceive or bear children. Many fertility clinics help parents conceive a baby through artifical means. In a process called **in vitro fertilization (IVF)**, sperm and egg cells are united outside the body. The tiny embryos that start to grow can be genetically tested before they are put back inside their mother, to make sure they are healthy. People who want to donate (give) eggs or sperm to infertile people can be genetically tested to make sure they do not carry genetic diseases.

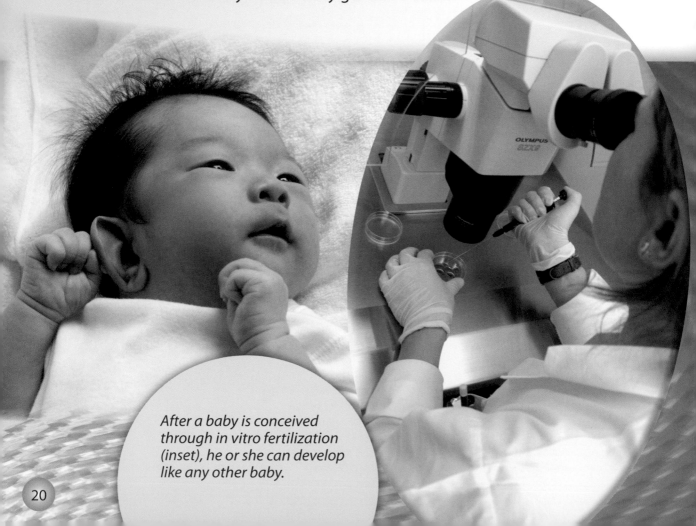

After a baby is conceived through in vitro fertilization (inset), he or she can develop like any other baby.

MORE QUESTIONS

When you read the term "designer baby", what comes to mind? Maybe you think of a baby who is designed like a living room, with any desired combination of traits. But this type of design is not possible, and wouldn't be even if it were legal. Many genetic techniques that are legal for mice and other animals are illegal for humans. And everything that is allowed is designed to result in a healthy baby.

Nevertheless, scientists and others are concerned about the real issues that genetic technology raises for the human race. The methods used to select healthy embryos could be used to choose the sex of a baby because the parents wanted a boy or a girl, not to avoid genetic diseases. Is this a good idea? Should parents be allowed to choose the colour of their baby's eyes even if it is possible? What if scientists could effectively test sperm and eggs for traits such as intelligence or musical ability? Should such tests even be performed? Questions like these could become important in your lifetime.

"I think it's very important that we not bury our head in the sand and pretend these advances are not happening."

—Dr. Jeffrey Steinberg, director of a fertility institute

GENETICALLY MODIFIED CROPS

Farmers are now growing a variety of **genetically modified (GM)** crops, especially in the United States. In Europe, however, opposition to GM crops is greater, and they are less common there. Companies that develop GM crops insist that their products are effectively identical to unmodified crops. Yet critics strongly disagree. The controversy continues, and the outcome will affect the world food supply for many years.

Many nations face shortages of food. Experts disagree about whether GM crops can help solve this problem.

ARGUMENTS FOR...

As you have read, genetic modification can help crop plants resist pests and drought (severe lack of rain). They can also be made to resist **herbicides**, which are chemicals that kill weeds.

In theory, these qualities make GM crops easier and more economical to grow. On a large farm, huge sums of money are invested to plant seeds and raise crops. In theory, GM crops help farmers receive a better return for their investment and labour, and ensure that the world receives food from the farm.

GM crops can also be made to be more nutritious. A GM strain of rice has been made to produce vitamin A. The future may bring other vitamin-enhanced crops.

...AND AGAINST

Critics argue that GM crops are not necessary, and that they are dangerous to both the environment and human health.

The techniques of **genetic technology** have been compared to performing heart surgery with a garden shovel. A transferred **gene** could affect an **organism** in unintended ways. The damage might take many generations to appear.

Critics cite studies that show that GM peas caused an allergic reaction in mice, evidence that genetic modification can change foods for the worse. Other studies suggest that GM foods are less nutritious than unmodified foods. Critics are also concerned that GM crops will breed with other crops, permanently changing them in unknown ways.

SAFETY CONCERNS

Look again at the photo shown on page 15. Genetic monsters like this one are not a real concern. Scientists also doubt that **genetic technology** could create a human monster, even if such technology were legal on humans. However, scientists have many real concerns about safety, especially from **GM** crops.

Bees spread pollen from flower to flower. They could spread genes from GM crops to wild plants.

Farms are not isolated from nature. GM plants can easily spread from the fields where they are grown.

GENETIC POLLUTION

Transgenic organisms could cause problems if their **genes** "escaped" into new **organisms**. This kind of gene spread is called **genetic pollution**.

When a GM crop is grown, it does not merely provide food for humans. Honeybees feed on the crop, as do birds and other wild animals. The genes could transfer to these animals, with unknown consequences.

GM crops also spread their new genes in **pollen**. Pollen has to go from one flower to another for plants to reproduce. Through insects, birds, and the wind, pollen can travel from crop plants to wild plants. New genes could easily enter the environment in this way. Again, no one is certain what the effect would be.

Unlike other kinds of pollution, genetic pollution may be impossible to clean up. Once a gene escapes into the wild, it might be there permanently.

Slow down?

The first GM crop, a variety of tomato, was introduced in 1994. Within a few years, many more crops were developed and raised. Many critics argue that long-term testing should have been conducted to determine the safety and value of these crops. They still want these tests conducted today.

ETHICAL ISSUES

Ethics is the study of right versus wrong. You have already read about many of these questions, and there are many more. As with other questions of ethics, the ethical questions raised by **genetic technology** are often difficult to answer. Sometimes an answer to one question leads to more questions that are even harder to answer.

IS IT RIGHT?

Is it right for humans to change the **genes** of plants and animals? Before you decide the answer, consider the fact that humans have always made such changes. This is how most of our familiar farm crops and animals came into existence.

In a process called **selective breeding**, a human breeder chooses parent plants or animals to mate. The parents have desirable **traits**, and these traits are passed to offspring. In this way, strains of corn have been bred for sweet, tasty kernels. Cattle have been bred for either their milk or meat.

People created blue roses using genetic technology. Some people have questioned the ethics of this.

Breeding has also created new kinds of animals. Donkeys and horses are mated to produce mules. People have also mated horses with zebras.

Dairy cattle are the result of many years of selective breeding.

THE ETHICAL DIFFERENCE

If selective breeding is acceptable, what might make genetic technology unacceptable? Does the fact that genetic technology involves scientists and laboratories make a difference? If a gene from **bacteria** could naturally transfer to a plant or animal, would that make it acceptable for scientists to perform the same transfer in laboratories?

As you consider these questions, remember that selective breeding still relies on chance. It also changes species in very limited ways. The genes of a fish and a plant would never mingle together in nature, but it could happen with genetic technology.

"[Genetic engineering] is a matter far too important to be left solely in the hands of the scientific and medical communities."

—*James D. Watson, co-discoverer of the structure of DNA*

HUMAN HEALTH

Genetic technology is now being used to create new medicines and therapies for many disorders and diseases. In the future, the impact of genetic technology may even be greater.

GENE THERAPY

A **genetic disorder** is a condition in which **genes** cause the body to function poorly. Some genetic disorders, such as Down's syndrome, arise when **chromosomes** form or develop abnormally. Other disorders are inherited, or come to a child from a parent's genes.

Cystic fibrosis is an inherited disorder that is caused by a single defective gene. This defective gene causes the body to produce very thick, sticky mucus. The mucus clogs the lungs and breathing passages.

To treat cystic fibrosis, scientists are now experimenting with **gene therapy**. Gene therapy is any technique that uses genes to treat a disease or disorder. Scientists are experimenting with ways to deliver the normal gene to a patient's lungs. The treatment is promising because it treats the cause of cystic fibrosis, not the symptoms.

THE RISKS OF GENE THERAPY

Like other experimental treatments on humans, gene therapy offers both rewards and risks. One risk comes from the **vector**, or carrier, of the gene that the patient receives. Viruses (tiny disease-causing **organisms**) might make ideal vectors, but they can also cause serious infections.

In 1999, 18-year-old Jesse Gelsinger became the first person to die in a test for gene therapy. Jesse suffered from a rare genetic disorder that affected the liver. He died because of his body's response to the virus used in the therapy.

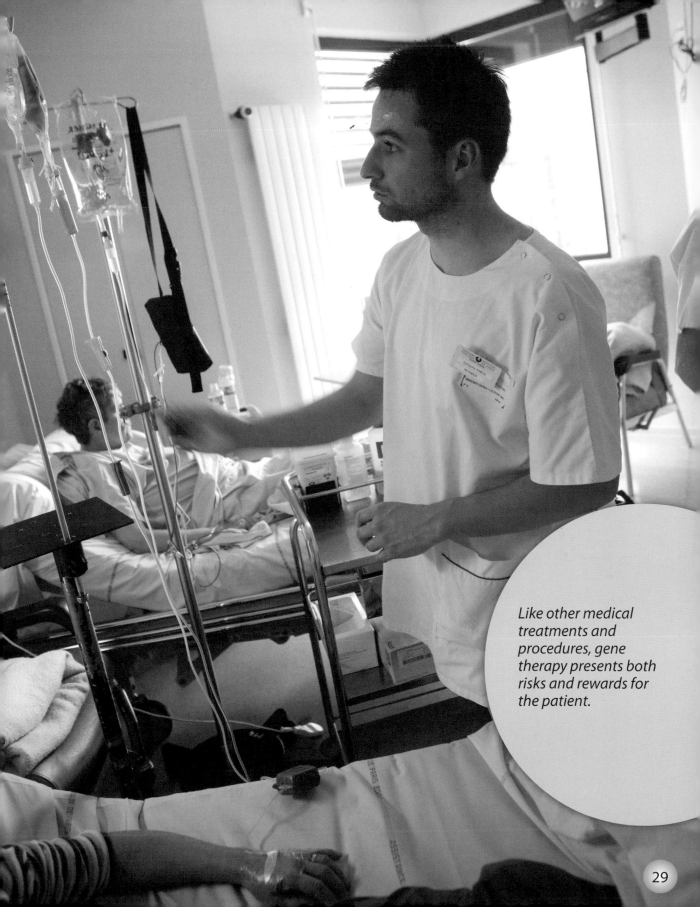

Like other medical treatments and procedures, gene therapy presents both risks and rewards for the patient.

CLONING

A **clone** is an exact genetic duplicate. Scientists have successfully cloned many animals, but also have had many failures. As cloning technology improves, cloned farm animals, pets, and wild animals may become very common. Not surprisingly, many people have strong opinions about whether cloning should be allowed – especially on humans.

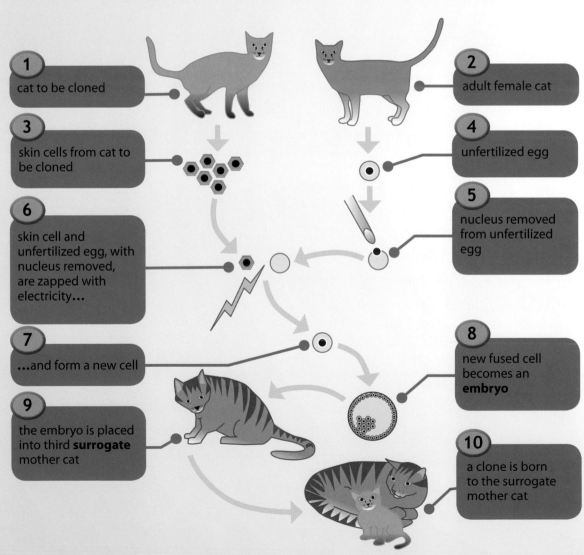

1 cat to be cloned

2 adult female cat

3 skin cells from cat to be cloned

4 unfertilized egg

5 nucleus removed from unfertilized egg

6 skin cell and unfertilized egg, with nucleus removed, are zapped with electricity...

7 ...and form a new cell

8 new fused cell becomes an **embryo**

9 the embryo is placed into third **surrogate** mother cat

10 a clone is born to the surrogate mother cat

DOLLY THE SHEEP

In 1996, after over 200 failed attempts, scientists succeeded in creating Dolly, a cloned sheep. Dolly was not the first cloned animal. But she was the first clone of an adult **mammal**. Her successful birth raised the possibility of cloning any adult animal for any purpose.

Dolly died in 2003. She lived a normal life that included giving birth to lambs. Although scientists have cloned other farm animals, cloning remains experimental and not practical.

HUMAN CLONING

With new technology, scientists can clone human **cells**. Now they hope to use cloned human cells to repair damaged body parts such as an injured spinal cord. In theory, cloned cells could also remake a whole body. A fertilized human egg that is cloned could grow and develop inside the mother's body, the same way any other human baby develops.

The cloning of humans is illegal in many nations. Many ethicists and religious leaders have criticized the entire concept. Do you agree? What is your opinion?

IT'S NOT SO EASY

At first glance, the technique for cloning seems simple. First, scientists take an egg from an animal and remove the genetic contents. Genes from the donor are then inserted, replacing the original genes, and a clone is made.

Yet for reasons scientists do not quite understand, this technique fails much more often than it succeeds. Dogs have proved especially hard to clone. Chickens and monkeys have proved even more difficult. Animals often die during the experiments.

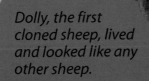

Dolly, the first cloned sheep, lived and looked like any other sheep.

31

DNA
FINGERPRINTING

As you now know, most **DNA** is the same from animal to animal. Among humans, nearly all DNA is the same. However, scientists have identified specific regions of DNA that differ from person to person. These differences are analyzed in a technique called **DNA fingerprinting**, which is used to identify people. DNA fingerprinting is used as evidence in court cases and to identify family relationships. The technology also raises many ethical and legal questions.

This researcher is examining information taken from DNA. Procedures like this can be used to find evidence that can be used in court.

EVIDENCE FROM DNA

Soon after a baby is born, hospital staff press the baby's hands or feet in ink and then make a print. Everyone has a unique set of whirls and ridges on his or her fingers and toes. The pattern can be used to identify each person.

DNA fingerprinting works in much the same way. Scientists can obtain DNA from blood or any tissue sample, such as skin. By comparing the DNA from two samples, they can determine whether or not the samples came from the same donor.

Evidence from DNA has led to guilty and not-guilty verdicts in many cases. Some people who have been in prison for 20 years or longer have had their innocence proven by DNA evidence.

Private property?

In the United States, the US military stores DNA samples of all soldiers and issues DNA-based identification tags. Security experts have suggested that DNA be used to identify civilians (people who aren't in the military), too.

Does your DNA belong to you? Is it completely private property, or does society have a right to register it? These questions may become very important in the years ahead.

GENES AND THE LAW

Are enough laws in place to regulate **genetic technology**? Do existing laws reflect the advances and discoveries of the technology? Many experts say the answer to both questions is no. Genetic technology is developing rapidly, perhaps faster than the laws that apply to it. Today, new discoveries are forcing judges to question the laws and rulings that made sense 20 or 30 years ago.

In the United States, GM foods are sold with no special labels or identification. Do you think the laws should be changed?

"Sugar, High Fructose Corn Syrup, Water,Enr[...]
Flour (Wheat Flour, Niacin, Reduced Iron, T'[...]
[Vitamin B1] Riboflavin [Vitamin B2] Folic [...]
Hydrogenated Soybean and Cottonseed O[...]
Preserve Flavor (Contributes a Trivial Amou[...]
Palm and Palm Kernel Oil, Dextrose, cocoa, Eg[...]
Oil, Colors (Caramel Color, Red 40) Emulsifiers (Sor[...]
Monostearate, Polysorbate 60, Mono- and Diglycerides, [...]
Soy Lecithin) Whey (Milk) Leavening (Baking Soda, Sodiu[...]
Aluminum Phosphate) Salt, Corn Starch, Sorbic Acid (to [...]
Retain Freshness) Natural and Artificial Flavors, Egg Whit[...]

Many consumers accept or reject a food based on its ingredients and preparation, including genetic modification.

A CHANGE TO PATENT LAWS

A **patent** is a legal document that gives an inventor the exclusive rights to an invention. Patents are important. Companies or individuals can invest time and money into their inventions because they know a patent will be available.

For many years, governments would not give patents for things found in nature. Then, in 1980, the US Supreme Court ruled in favour of Ananda Chakrabarty, a scientist who had developed an **organism** for cleaning oil spills. This was the first time any government had granted a patent for a living organism. Since then, courts all over the world have granted thousands of patents for **genes** and **transgenic organisms**.

In the 1980 decision, one of the key science arguments was that genes had very predictable effects, and these effects stayed the same from organism to organism. Scientists now know that this idea is incorrect. The same gene may operate in different ways in a bacterium, a plant, and an animal. Nevertheless, patents for individual genes continue to be granted.

Seeds in court

Monsanto is an international company that makes and sells GM seeds. The company has accused many farmers of stealing these seeds. The farmers insist that the seeds drifted into their fields from neighbouring farms. They are accusing Monsanto of genetic pollution!

In California, a new law is helping to protect the farmers' rights. But the controversy continues.

GENES AND THE FUTURE

Scientists continue to make discoveries and breakthroughs in **genetic technology**. As genetic technology advances and becomes more widespread, its impact on society will continue to increase. Here are four examples of issues that could become very important in the future. Some are already important today!

GM FOOD ANIMALS

Many animals have been **genetically modified (GM)**. Most are either kept in laboratories, such as **knockout** mice, or used for **pharming**, such as the sheep which make blood clotting proteins in their milk. Now scientists have created GM salmon. If approved, the salmon would be the first GM animal to be used for food.

The AquAdvantage® Salmon has **genes** that allow it to grow faster and larger than other salmon. The company that owns the **patent** claims that the salmon's eggs are infertile, meaning they will not hatch. But some scientists dispute this claim.

Questions

Is GM salmon safe to eat? Could its altered genes escape into fish populations in the wild? If so, how would those populations change?

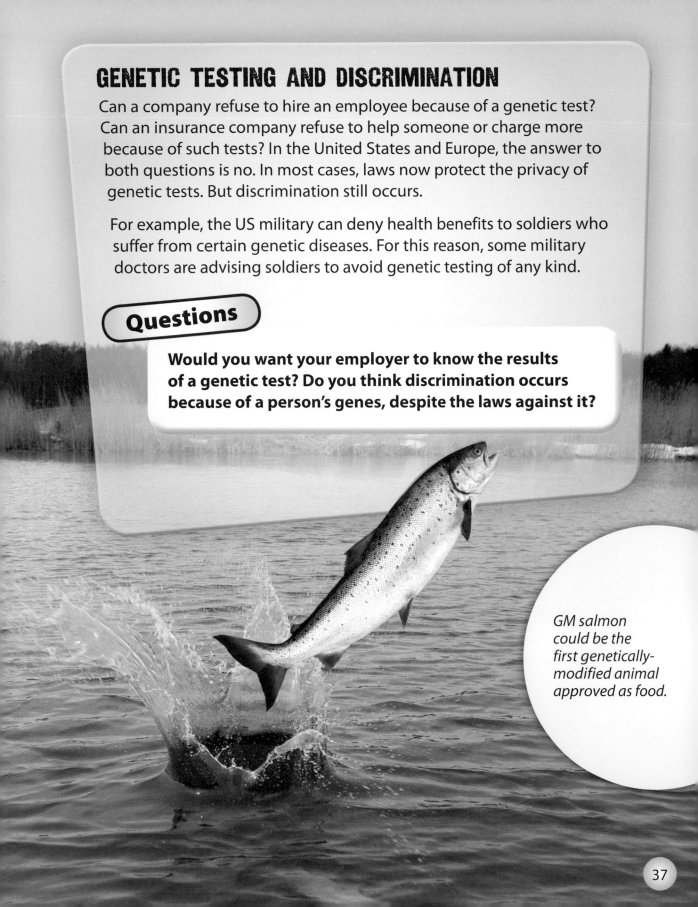

GENETIC TESTING AND DISCRIMINATION

Can a company refuse to hire an employee because of a genetic test? Can an insurance company refuse to help someone or charge more because of such tests? In the United States and Europe, the answer to both questions is no. In most cases, laws now protect the privacy of genetic tests. But discrimination still occurs.

For example, the US military can deny health benefits to soldiers who suffer from certain genetic diseases. For this reason, some military doctors are advising soldiers to avoid genetic testing of any kind.

Questions

Would you want your employer to know the results of a genetic test? Do you think discrimination occurs because of a person's genes, despite the laws against it?

GM salmon could be the first genetically-modified animal approved as food.

EPIGENETICS

Humans have around 20,000 to 25,000 genes. But different sets of genes are active in every **cell**, and different genes are active at different times. **Epigenetics** is the study of how factors in the environment can affect genes. These factors include diet and stress.

By studying epigenetics, scientists hope to develop drugs that could "turn off" the genes that play a role in diseases. The drugs could help treat diseases such as cancer, autism, and Alzheimer's.

The study of epigenetics has already provided evidence for a new idea about genetic inheritance. As scientists know very well, people can shorten their lives with behaviours such as heavy smoking or over-eating. Yet these actions also affect the genes, and the genetic damage can pass from parent to child.

Questions

Should scientists pursue genetic treatments for diseases?

Azacitidine, shown here in crystallized form, is the first epigenetic drug.

STEM CELL RESEARCH

More than 100 trillion cells make up the adult human body. These cells are highly specialized, meaning they have different structures that let them do different jobs. Cells in muscle tissue, for example, look different and function differently than cells in bones and the blood.

In contrast, cells that appear very early in development are not differentiated. These are **stem cells**, the cells that grow into the wide variety and huge number of cells in the body.

Scientists around the world are now studying stem cells and how their genes function. The hope is that stem cells could help humans regrow injured or lost cells, such as from brain or spinal cord injuries. But stem cell research is controversial. Useful stem cells come from early stages of human life. Not everyone agrees that stem cell research is ethical.

Questions

What do you think about the ethics of stem cell research?

If damaged nerves could be regenerated, this basketball player could walk again.

CHANGING THE RULES

For many years, scientists thought that the chemicals of living things behaved very differently from other chemicals. Then, in 1828, German chemist Friedrich Wohler synthesized (made) **urea** in his laboratory. Urea is the waste product that the liver makes. Scientists of the time thought that Wohler's accomplishment was impossible!

Today, **genetic technology** has led to many events that were once thought impossible. Corn plants are making their own pesticides. **Bacteria** are making human **insulin**. Parents can choose the gender of their child to avoid terrible genetic diseases. Many rules about life that once seemed valid no longer apply.

...TO WHAT END?

So what comes next? What old rules about life will scientists discover can be broken? And what benefits or drawbacks will these discoveries bring? Only time will tell.

Whether or not you become a scientist, your opinion matters about the direction of science and technology. Scientists will continue to study and investigate how **organisms** live, grow, and function. Whether this knowledge should be developed into new technology, and how such technology should be used, are issues for everyone in society to decide.

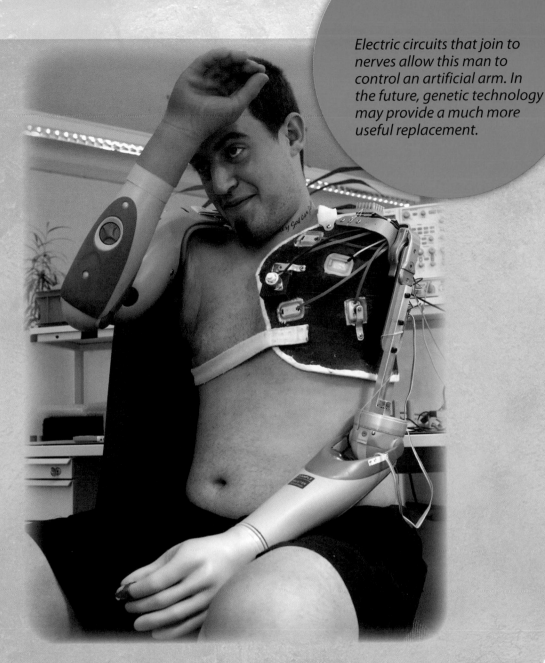

Electric circuits that join to nerves allow this man to control an artificial arm. In the future, genetic technology may provide a much more useful replacement.

ARTIFICIAL LIMBS

Years ago, an artificial arm or leg was merely a stick of wood or plastic. Today, such limbs are highly technical devices. In many cases, the person can use his or her nervous system to control the motion of the limb. Nevertheless, even the most advanced artificial limb is less useful than the original.

Could the body be made to regrow a lost limb? Or could nerves be regrown and trained to operate an artificial limb? Genetic technology could make this possible.

SUMMARY

Genetic technology is a rapidly developing branch of science. Major advances have been made within the past 20 years. Many more advances are likely in the near future.

Scientists have now created dozens of **transgenic organisms**, meaning they have transferred **genes** from one organism to another. Transgenic farm crops have been made with genes from other plants and **bacteria** that provide resistance to pests and drought. Transgenic microorganisms, plants, and animals have been made with genes from the human body for useful products, such as **insulin**.

Although altering human genes is illegal, genetic technology is used to analyze human genes and predict genetic **traits**. Experiments on mice show how human genes function. The results could lead to new treatments for diseases and for **genetic disorders**.

Yet genetic technology is not without risks and drawbacks. Many people argue that GM food crops are harmful to the environment and human health. Many people also object to all types of genetic technology for ethical reasons.

RESEARCH TOPICS

Look online or in printed reference sources for information on these topics. If you want to find out more about genetic technology, try researching some of these topics.

DNA, here shown in a model, is the basis of all genetic technology.

NEW TRANSGENIC ORGANISMS
GM plants and animals are being developed every day. Some are intended for laboratory research, others for the supermarket. Search for transgenic bacteria, transgenic sheep, transgenic mice or transgenic plants.

NEW GENE THERAPIES Scientists continue studying **gene therapies** for treating **genetic disorders**. Research their progress in cystic fibrosis or SCID gene therapy.

NEW LAWS AND COURT CASES All over the world, governments are debating laws that affect **genetic technology** and its use. Search for laws, judges, and genetic technology.

NEW DISCOVERIES Scientists continue studying the **DNA** and **genes** of humans and other **organisms**. Their discoveries can overturn old ideas. Search for genetic technology discoveries.

NEW CONCERNS Scientists, government leaders, and citizens groups continue to evaluate genetic technology and its consequences. Search for genetic technology **ethics**.

Glossary

bacteria single-celled microorganism

base basic unit that makes up DNA

cell smallest parts, or building blocks, of a plant or animal

chromosome structure that contains genes; carried in the cell nucleus

clone exact genetic duplicate of an organism

diabetes disease in which the body does not make or process insulin appropriately

DNA deoxyribonucleic acid, the molecule that codes for traits in all organisms

DNA fingerprinting technique in which DNA is analyzed to identify an individual

embryo tiny bundle of cells, that is formed in the first few days of a new human's or animal's development

epigenetics study of how the environment affects genes and gene expression

ethics study of right and wrong

fertilization process of an egg cell joining with a sperm cell, creating the potential for an embryo to develop in the right conditions

fertility ability to have children or offspring

gene part of the genetic information of a living thing. Most genes tell cells how to make a particular protein.

gene therapy use of genetic technology to treat a disease or illness

genetic counselling providing information about genes and helping people make decisions that relate to genes

genetic disorder illness or condition caused by atypical genes

genetic pollution spread of harmful or unwanted genes into the wild

genetic technology change or study of an organism's genes for a useful purpose

genetically modified (GM) genes that have been artificially altered

herbicide chemical that kills weeds or other small plants

in vitro fertilization (IVF) joining of egg and sperm in an artificial environment, such as a test tube

insulin chemical the body makes to help control blood sugar levels

knockout organism from which one gene was removed

mammal warm-blooded animal that makes milk for its young

molecule group of atoms bonded together

nerve body tissue that transmits electrical signals

nucleus membrane-bound structure in the cell that contains chromosomes

organism individual living thing

patent legal document that provides the rights to an invention

pharming using genetically-modified organisms to produce drugs or medicines

pollen powder that plants make to reproduce

selective breeding choosing parents with desired traits to mate

stem cell cell that can divide to produce very specific cells, such as nerve cells

surrogate female who carries a developing fetus, which has been created using an egg cell from a different female

trait characteristic or feature of an organism

transgenic organism organism made from transferred genes

transgenic plant plant to which one or more genes were added from another organism

urea waste product of animals

vector organism that carries and transmits a virus or other agent of disease

Find out more

Books

Body Doubles: Cloning Plants and Animals (Science at the Edge) by Sally Morgan (Heinemann Library, 2009)

Decoding Genes with Max Axiom (Graphic Science) by Amber Keyser (Capstone Press, 2010)

DNA and Genetic Engineering (Cells & Life) by Robert Snedden (Heinemann Library, 2007)

Evolution Revolution by Robert Winston (DK Publishing, 2009)

Genetic Engineering (Cool Science) by Ron Fridell (Lerner Publications, 2006)

Using Genetic Technology (Why Science Matters) by Andrew Solway (Heinemann Library, 2008)

What Makes Me, Me? by Robert Winston (DK Publishing, 2009)

What's Biology All About? by Hazell Maskell and Adam Larkum (Usborne Publishing, 2009)

Websites

www.iptv.org/exploremore/ge
From Iowa Public Television comes this companion website to a television documentary.

www.dnai.org
This website is devoted to DNA: how it was discovered, how it works, and how it affects your life.

www.sciencemuseum.org.uk/WhoAmI/FindOutMore/Yourgenes.aspx
This website shows an animated explanation of how and why your genes make you unique.

http://kidshealth.org/teen
Search this website for articles on genes, genetic disorders, or any other health topic that interests you.

www.eurekascience.com
Click the links on this website to learn about DNA, cloning, and other science topics.

http://learn.genetics.utah.edu/content/tech/cloning
This site provides interactive introductions to cloning. You can even try it yourself in the mouse cloning laboratory.

Index

            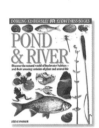  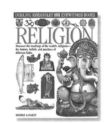                  

MYTHOLOGY

Monstrous chimera

Maori ceremonial adze (ax)

Hideous Gorgon Medusa

Ritual sword used in Ogun worship

The Wealthy One (1988), a contemporary Native American mask

Hindu animal god Garuda

Mold and casting of Venus, Roman goddess of love

Tibetan *vajras*, representing thunderbolts of the gods

DK EYEWITNESS BOOKS

MYTHOLOGY

Written by
NEIL PHILIP

Maori bird-man kite

Native American shaman

Dorling Kindersley

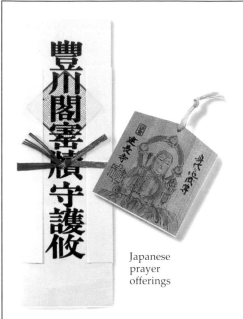

African fortune-telling cowrie shells

Japanese prayer offerings

Dorling Kindersley
LONDON, NEW YORK, DELHI, JOHANNESBURG, MUNICH, PARIS and SYDNEY

For a full catalog, visit

DK www.dk.com

Project editor Melanie Halton
Art editor Joanne Connor
Senior managing editor Linda Martin
Senior managing art editor Julia Harris
Production Kate Oliver
Picture research Andy Sansom
DTP designer Andrew O'Brien
Jacket designer Dean Price

This Eyewitness ® Book has been conceived by
Dorling Kindersley Limited and Editions Gallimard

© 1999 Dorling Kindersley Limited
This edition © 2000 Dorling Kindersley Limited
First American edition, 1999

Published in the United States by
Dorling Kindersley Publishing, Inc.
95 Madison Avenue
New York, NY 10016
4 6 8 10 9 7 5 3

Dorling Kindersley books are available at special discounts for bulk purchases for sales promotions or premiums. Special editions, including personalized covers, excerpts of existing guides, and corporate imprints can be created in large quantities for specific needs. For more information, contact Special Markets Dept., Dorling Kindersley Publishing, Inc., 95 Madison Ave., New York, NY 10016; Fax: (800) 600-9098

Library of Congress Cataloging-in-Publication Data
Philip, Neil.
Mythology / written by Neil Philip.
p. cm. — (Eyewitness Books) Includes index.
Summary: Surveys the treatment of gods, goddesses, the heavens, creation, death, and evil as expressed in various mythologies around the world.
1. Mythology — Juvenile literature. 2. Religions — Juvenile literature.
[1. Mythology.] I. Title.
BL311.P485 2000 291.1'3—dc21 98–32234
ISBN 0-7894-6289-3 (pb)   ISBN 0-7894-6288-5 (hc)

Color reproduction by Colourscan, Singapore
Printed in China by Toppan Printing Co. (Shenzhen) Ltd.

Oceanic ceremonial ax

Staff representing African thunder god Shango's ax

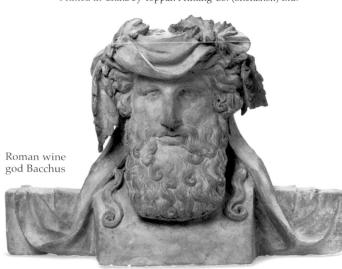

Roman wine god Bacchus

Tangaroa, supreme god of Polynesia

Back of Tangaroa

Contents

Native American Navajo sand painting

Sand painting pigments

What is mythology?

THE WORD "MYTH" comes from the Greek "mythos," meaning a legend or a story. Sometimes it is used to mean something people believe that is not true: "It's a myth that carrots help you see in the dark." But mythology is not a collection of lies; it is a collection of truths. Each human culture makes stories about the creation of the world, the origins of humankind, and the meaning of life. These stories are myths. In one sense, mythology is religion in story form. But while the essence of religious belief is usually very simple, mythology can be highly complex. This is because myths are stories that explore rather than explain. They show the human mind searching to balance the forces of creation and destruction, of life and death.

Longhaired figures represent the shaman wrestling with the beaver

CREATION OF THE WORLD
Numerous mythologies tell how the creator emerged from a cosmic egg or a primordial (existing from the beginning) ocean. The world was then brought into being, perhaps from the creator's own body, perhaps from mud, or even by the power of words or thought. The first Hindu god, Brahma, is sometimes said to have been born from a golden egg that floated on the first waters.

Hindu creation symbol

Myth beginnings

Humankind has made myths from the dawn of history. The oldest living mythology is that of the Australian Aborigines, whose stories of the sacred eternal Dreamtime stretch back 40,000 years. The myths of diverse cultures are often linked by similar themes. This time line shows the approximate dates that individual societies began recording or shaping their myths.

Burning stick symbolizes the beaver's magic powers

40,000 B.C.	10,000 B.C.		4,000 B.C.	3,000 B.C.	2,000 B.C.	
		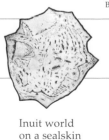			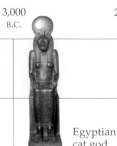	
Aboriginal Dreamtime tools	African god Eshu	Inuit world on a sealskin	Sumerian winged bull	Egyptian cat god Sekhmet	Chinese war god Guan Di	Aztec god Quetzalcoatl

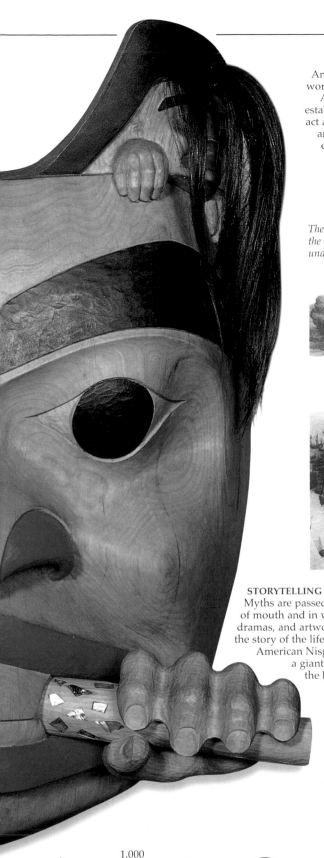

GUIDING ANCESTORS

Ancestors play an important role in world mythology. For the Australian Aborigines, the laws and customs established by ancestor spirits (right) act as guidelines for life today. These ancestors exist outside time, in the eternal present of the Dreamtime. Aboriginal myths are stories of the Dreamtime, and Aboriginal art and ceremonies are ways of connecting with the ancestors.

The Tower of Babel fell when the workmen could no longer understand each other

CHALLENGING THE GODS

Not all are content to worship the gods; some even challenge them. When Nimrod, King of Babylon, built a tower to reach Heaven and make war on God, God sent 70 angels to confuse the builders' tongues. Some say that this is why people now speak different languages.

STORYTELLING

Myths are passed on by storytelling, not only by word of mouth and in writing, but also in rituals, dances, dramas, and artworks. This medicine beaver mask tells the story of the life-or-death struggle between a North American Nisga-a shaman, or medicine man, and a giant beaver, in which the shaman made the beaver into his spirit helper.

DEATH AND AFTERLIFE

Many mythologies hope for a new life after death. The Egyptians and the Greeks both linked the idea of an afterlife with the annual death and resurrection of corn. The Greeks worshiped Persephone (right), daughter of the corn goddess Demeter, queen of the dead, in rites that they believed held the entire human race together.

1,000 B.C.					1 A.D.		1,000 A.D.

Hindu god Garuda

Bible story of Adam and Eve

Polynesian god Tangaroa

Greek supreme god Zeus

Celtic horned god Cernunnos

Roman war god Mars

Norse god Thor's hammer

Japanese prayers

Creation of the world

COSMIC EGG
A bird-man from Easter Island is shown holding the cosmic egg that contains the world. Each year in the nesting season on Easter Island, the man whose servant was the first to gather an egg became the Bird Man, the living representative for that year of the creator god Makemake.

MANY PEOPLES seem to agree that this world was made as a deliberate act of creation by a divine being. Often the world is described as having originally been all ocean, and it is from the sea that the world emerges in the earliest mythologies. Nun was the god of the Egyptian primal ocean. The Arctic Tikigak people say that Raven made the land by harpooning a great whale, which then floated and became dry land. Sometimes there are two creators, who together shape the world, such as First Creator and Lone Man of the Native American Mandan tribe. They sent a mud hen down to fetch mud from the bottom of the flood to make the first land.

FIRE AND ICE
The Vikings believed that the world began when fire from the south met ice from the north. At the center, the ice began to thaw and, as it dripped, it shaped itself into the first being, Ymir, whose sweat formed the first frost giants. Then the ice-melt shaped a cow, whose milk fed Ymir. As the cow licked the ice, she shaped the first man, Buri.

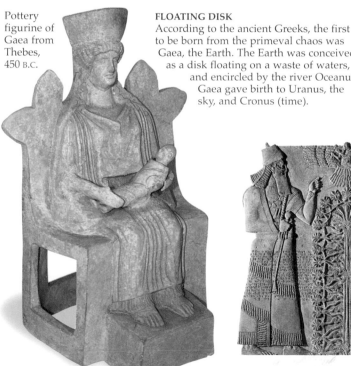

Pottery figurine of Gaea from Thebes, 450 B.C.

FLOATING DISK
According to the ancient Greeks, the first to be born from the primeval chaos was Gaea, the Earth. The Earth was conceived as a disk floating on a waste of waters, and encircled by the river Oceanus. Gaea gave birth to Uranus, the sky, and Cronus (time).

Ahura Mazda, from the tree of life relief, 9th century B.C.

THE BIG BANG
Scientists now say that the world began with the big bang, a huge explosion 10 billion years ago that sent matter in all directions to create the ever-expanding universe. This is a new vision of beginning, a new "myth" for a scientific age.

CREATED FROM GOODNESS
The ancient Persians believed in twin spirits who had existed since the beginning of time: Ahura Mazda, who was good; and Ahriman, who was evil. It was Ahura Mazda who created the physical world, set time in motion, and created humankind.

TURTLE ISLAND
Many Native Americans believe that this world is supported on a turtle's back. According to the Seneca tribe, when the first woman fell down from another world in the sky, the toad that lived on the primal waters dived down to fetch mud to place on the turtle's back. The mud, which became Earth, provided support for the first woman.

The first land was said to have been created on a turtle's back

19th-century Native American Cheyenne shield

CURDLING OCEAN
The Japanese god Izanagi and his wife Izanami stood on the floating bridge of heaven and stirred the ocean with a jeweled spear until it curdled and formed the first island, Onokoro. They built a house there, with a central stone pillar that is the backbone of the world.

Vishnu sits on top of Mount Mandara

OCEAN CHURNING
At the beginning of this cycle of creation, a number of vital treasures, including the elixir of immortality, were not to be found, so the Hindu gods decided to churn the ocean, using Mount Mandara as the paddle. As they churned, the ocean turned to milk, then to butter, and the sun and moon arose. As they churned some more, the elixir was finally created.

Vasuki, the cosmic serpent, was used as a rope to twist the mountain

The mountain is supported by a giant turtle

The Milky Way and the planets of the Solar System. Clockwise from the bottom are the Earth, Mars, Jupiter, Saturn, Uranus, and Neptune.

The cosmos

PEOPLE HAVE ALWAYS WONDERED about the mysteries of the world, from its origin and shape to its cosmos, or order. The world is often thought to have emerged from a cosmic egg. In China, the warring forces of yin and yang in the egg created the first being, Pan Gu. The Dogon of West Africa believe the world was formed from a vibrating egg that burst open to reveal a creator spirit. The Ainu of Japan believed there were six skies above this Earth and six worlds below it, the abodes of gods, demons, and animals. The world has long been thought of as round. A myth told by the Inuit people of the Arctic tundra tells how two families set out in opposite directions to discover how big the world is. When they met up again, they were very old, but the fact that they came back to where they started proved that the world is round. The Mangaian people of Polynesia say that the universe is held in the shell of a huge coconut.

Inuit people of the Arctic tundra build an igloo, which is round like the world

WORLD IN A SEALSKIN

On this sealskin painted by the Chukchi people of Siberia, the whole world — sun, moon, land, sea, and sky — is captured in a small space. In this sealskin world, human beings share creation with spirits, animals, and gods such as the creator Raven and his wife, Miti, and Sedna, the mother of the sea beasts.

YIN AND YANG

The Chinese believed that the first being, Pan Gu, was created inside a cosmic egg by the opposing forces of yin and yang. When at last the conflict between yin and yang broke the egg open, Pan Gu was born and pushed the sky away from the Earth.

After he died, exhausted by this labor, his body formed the mountains and the land — and his fleas became humankind.

Yin and yang symbolize universal opposites, such as good and evil, that must be equally balanced for a harmonious world

Brahma, the creator of the Universe, is shown on Vishnu's forehead

Vishnu's conch shell symbolizes the very first vibration of the Universe — the sound "om"

The discus symbolizes the mind and the sun

WORLD TREE

For the Vikings the nine worlds, including humankind's "middle Earth," were arranged in three layers around the huge ash tree Yggdrasil, which stands at the center of the cosmos. The Vikings believed that the worlds of gods, giants, elves, dwarfs, humans, and the dead were all sustained by the world tree.

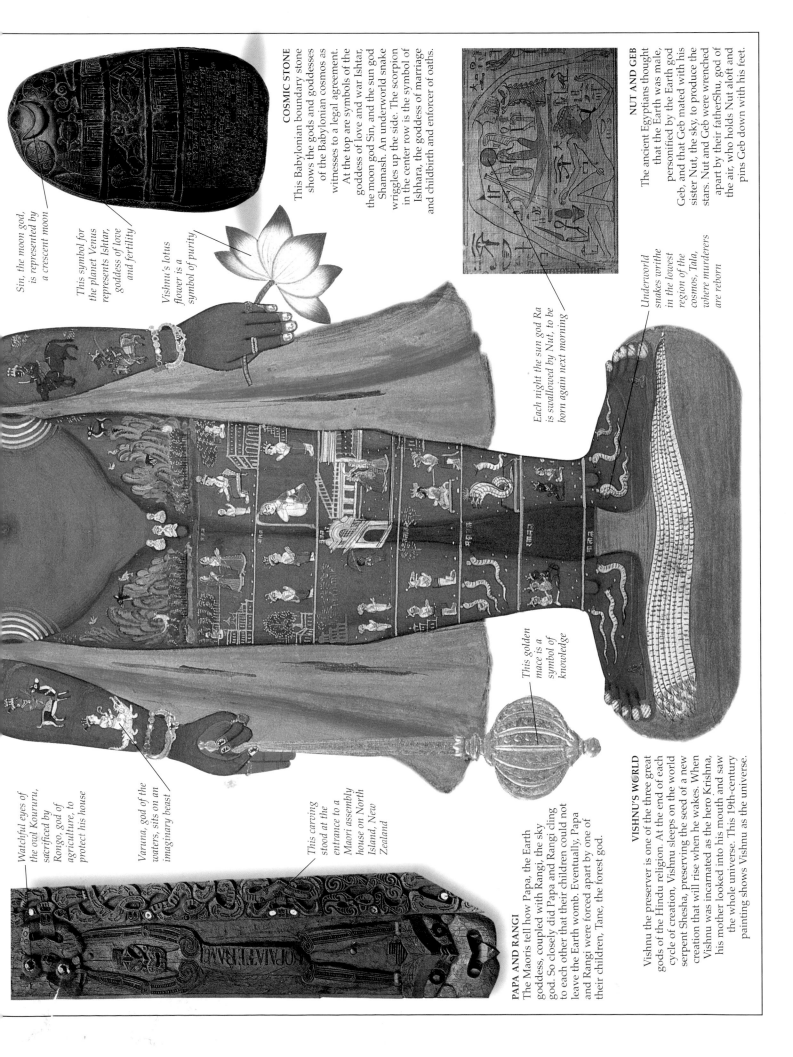

COSMIC STONE

This Babylonian boundary stone shows the gods and goddesses of the Babylonian cosmos as witnesses to a legal agreement. At the top are symbols of the goddess of love and war Ishtar, the moon god Sin, and the sun god Shamash. An underworld snake wriggles up the side. The scorpion in the center row is the symbol of Ishhara, the goddess of marriage and childbirth and enforcer of oaths.

Sin, the moon god, is represented by a crescent moon

This symbol for the planet Venus represents Ishtar, goddess of love and fertility

Vishnu's lotus flower is a symbol of purity

NUT AND GEB

The ancient Egyptians thought that the Earth was male, personified by the Earth god Geb, and that Geb mated with his sister Nut, the sky, to produce the stars. Nut and Geb were wrenched apart by their fatherShu, god of the air, who holds Nut aloft and pins Geb down with his feet.

Each night the sun god Ra is swallowed by Nut, to be born again next morning

Underworld snakes writhe in the lowest region of the cosmos, Tala, where murderers are reborn

Watchful eyes of the owl Koururu, sacrificed by Rongo, god of agriculture, to protect his house

Varuna, god of the waters, sits on an imaginary beast

This carving stood at the entrance to a Maori assembly house on North Island, New Zealand

This golden mace is a symbol of knowledge

PAPA AND RANGI

The Maoris tell how Papa, the Earth goddess, coupled with Rangi, the sky god. So closely did Papa and Rangi cling to each other that their children could not leave the Earth womb. Eventually, Papa and Rangi were forced apart by one of their children, Tane, the forest god.

VISHNU'S WORLD

Vishnu the preserver is one of the three great gods of the Hindu religion. At the end of each cycle of creation, Vishnu sleeps on the world serpent Shesha, preserving the seed of a new creation that will rise when he wakes. When Vishnu was incarnated as the hero Krishna, his mother looked into his mouth and saw the whole universe. This 19th-century painting shows Vishnu as the universe.

Sun and Moon

THE SUN AND THE MOON, which light up the sky by day and night and enable us to tell the time, have been the subject of many myths. For the Native American Zuni people, Moonlight-Giving Mother and Sun Father are the givers of light and life. The Native American Cherokees say the sun is female and tell of her grief when her daughter died from a rattlesnake bite. Sun hid herself away, the world grew dark, and her tears caused a flood. Only the dancing and singing of young men and women could cheer her up. The Arctic Chukchi tell how a woman married the sun, but a black beetle took her place; it was only when her son sought out his father that the imposter was discovered. Another Chukchi woman married the moon; she had been deserted by her husband and left to starve, but she crawled to moon's house and became his wife.

DEALER OF DAYS
The moon god Thoth was in charge of the Egyptian calendar, which had 12 months with 30 days each. The sky goddess Nut, who had been cursed so that she could never give birth, won five extra days from Thoth in which she had her children.

THE ROMAN MOON GODDESS DIANA
Diana (Artemis in Greek) is shown here with her foot resting on the moon, with which she was closely associated. More often, however, she is depicted with a crescent moon in her hair.

Diana as a crowned moon goddess

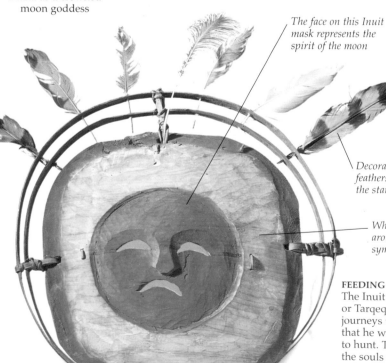

The face on this Inuit mask represents the spirit of the moon

Decorative feathers represent the stars

White border around the face symbolizes air

FEEDING HUMANKIND
The Inuit moon man is called Igaluk or Tarqeq. Shamans make spirit journeys to ask him to promise that he will send animals for men to hunt. The moon man also helps the souls of the dead to be reborn as humans, animals, or fish.

Painted moon face sculpted in wood

Native American Haida mask

POLLUTING THE WORLD
A Native American Haida myth tells how Wultcixaiya, the son of the moon, rescued his sister from her unhappy marriage to Pestilence. Wearing a steel coat, he broke into Pestilence's house of rock, freeing her, but also polluting the world with sickness and disease.

14

RA, THE SUN GOD
The falcon-headed god Horus
joined forces with the Egyptian sun
god Ra and became Ra-Horakhty.
He sailed a special boat, the
"solar bark," across the sky
by day and through the
underworld by night.

*The sun's
rays beam
down on a
worshiper*

*Projections
symbolize the
sun's rays*

INCA INTI
Viracocha, the Inca
creator god, ordered
the sun, moon, and stars
to emerge from the Island
of the Sun, in Lake Titicaca,
to bring light to the world.
Inti, the sun god, was regarded
as the father of the Inca emperors,
and his wife, Mama Kilya, the
moon goddess, as the mother
of the Inca race.

Pre-Columbian
gold sun mask,
300 B.C.

Tsimshian chief's
ceremonial headdress
representing the sun

CHILDREN OF THE SUN
The Native American Tsimshian hero Asdiwal was a
great hunter, who pursued a bear right up to the sky. The bear
turned out to be the sun's beautiful daughter, whom Asdiwal
married. The sun also has a son, a shining prince of the sky,
who had a constant battle of wits with his cheeky servant.

*The fertility
goddess Ishtar*

*Ea, the
water god*

*Shamash rising
between two
mountains*

*Amaterasu
holds the
imperial sword
and necklace*

ENEMY OF DARKNESS
The Babylonian sun god Shamash was the
only being able to cross the ocean of death,
until the hero Gilgamesh. Shamash was
a lawgiver and healer, the enemy of
darkness, wrongdoing, and disease.

THE SUN GODDESS AMATERASU
The Japanese sun goddess Amaterasu was so
offended by her brother Susano's practical
jokes that she hid in a cave and deprived
the world of the sun. Uzume, the goddess of
mirth, did a striptease and made the other
gods laugh. Intrigued, Amaterasu emerged
from the cave, returning sunlight to the world.

15

Making humankind

SNAKE GODDESS
Nü Wa, the first Chinese goddess, had the face of a girl but the body of a snake. She was lonely, so she made the first human beings out of mud and water to cheer herself up.

ALL MYTHOLOGIES TELL how the first human beings were made. Often the creator shaped them from clay or mud. The Unalit (North Alaskan Inuit) say that the first man was born from the pod of a beach pea. When he burst out of the pod, he was met by Raven, who taught him how to live and made him a wife out of clay. The Egyptians believed that the first human beings were made from the tears of Ra, the sun god. For the Serbians, people were made from the creator's sweat, which is why they say we are doomed to a life of toil. The Norse god Odin made the first man and woman from driftwood, but there is also a myth telling how the Norse god Heimdall fathered the various kinds of men: serfs, warriors, and kings.

Brahma has four heads so that he can see in all directions

BRAHMA THE CREATOR
The Hindu creator Brahma is the universal soul, the "self-existent great-grandfather." He made the world and everything in it. He is sometimes called Purusha, the first being. As Purusha he divided himself into two, male and female, and coupled in the form of every creature, from humans to ants.

Tangaroa brings forth other beings

Carved wooden bowl from the Yoruba in West Africa

The cosmic serpent Aido-Hwedo coiled itself around the Earth

BODIES OF CLAY
The West African creator Mawu made the first people from clay and water. The first man and woman, sometimes called Adanhu and Yewa, were sent down from the sky with the rainbow serpent Aido-Hwedo. For the first 17 days it did nothing but rain; the man and woman did not speak but only called out the name of the god who had sent them to Earth.

Adunhu

Yewa

Wooden statue from the Tubuaï Islands in Polynesia, where the supreme god Tangaroa is called A'a

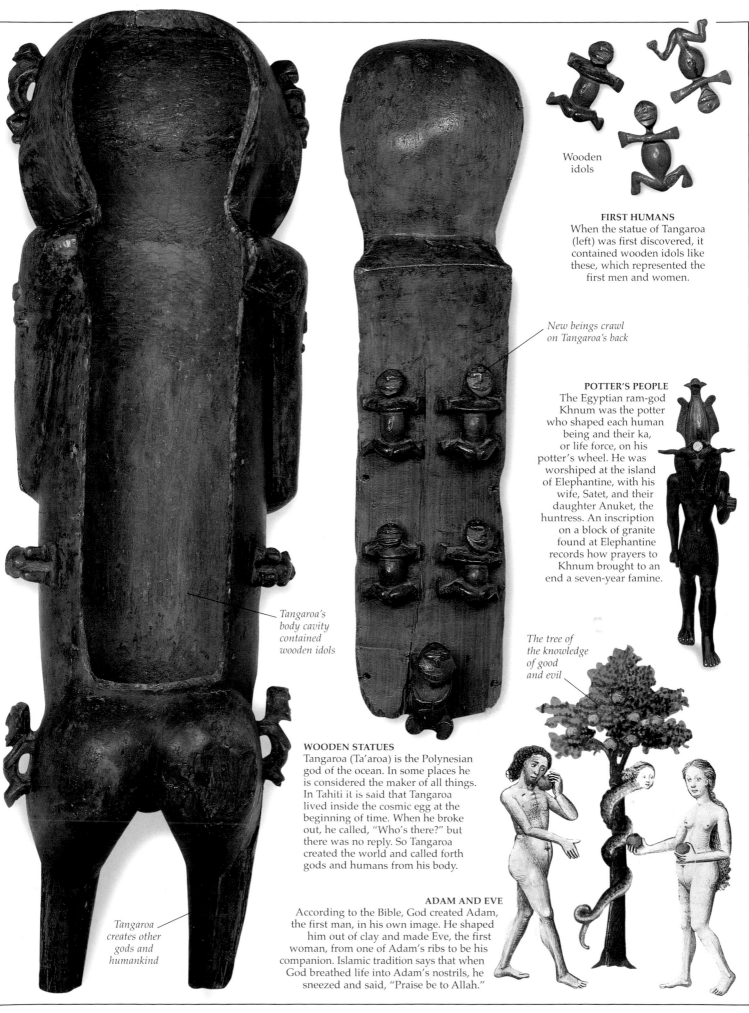

Wooden
idols

FIRST HUMANS
When the statue of Tangaroa
(left) was first discovered, it
contained wooden idols like
these, which represented the
first men and women.

*New beings crawl
on Tangaroa's back*

POTTER'S PEOPLE
The Egyptian ram-god
Khnum was the potter
who shaped each human
being and their ka,
or life force, on his
potter's wheel. He was
worshiped at the island
of Elephantine, with his
wife, Satet, and their
daughter Anuket, the
huntress. An inscription
on a block of granite
found at Elephantine
records how prayers to
Khnum brought to an
end a seven-year famine.

*Tangaroa's
body cavity
contained
wooden idols*

*The tree of
the knowledge
of good
and evil*

WOODEN STATUES
Tangaroa (Ta'aroa) is the Polynesian
god of the ocean. In some places he
is considered the maker of all things.
In Tahiti it is said that Tangaroa
lived inside the cosmic egg at the
beginning of time. When he broke
out, he called, "Who's there?" but
there was no reply. So Tangaroa
created the world and called forth
gods and humans from his body.

*Tangaroa
creates other
gods and
humankind*

ADAM AND EVE
According to the Bible, God created Adam,
the first man, in his own image. He shaped
him out of clay and made Eve, the first
woman, from one of Adam's ribs to be his
companion. Islamic tradition says that when
God breathed life into Adam's nostrils, he
sneezed and said, "Praise be to Allah."

17

Supreme beings

Thunderbolts were made for Zeus by the Cyclopes, giants who helped in the war against Zeus's father

MOST MYTHOLOGIES tell of one god who reigns supreme over all others. These supreme gods may be associated with the creation of the world and humankind. Many supreme deities, such as the Greek god Zeus, are essentially sky gods; others may be sun, battle, city, or tribal gods. In some cultures, especially in Africa, the supreme god is thought to have retired from the world after the initial creation. This is the case with Nana-Buluku, the creator deity of the Fon of West Africa; and with Nyame of the West African Ashanti people. Over time such gods may be almost forgotten. For instance, Nana-Buluku's daughter Mawu is now routinely described as the creator, and the word "mawu" has come to mean "god" in Fon.

Made of bronze and decorated with silver, this late Bronze Age figure represents the storm god Baal

RULER OF THE GREEKS
Zeus (known as Jupiter to the Romans) was ruler of the Greek gods. Zeus overthrew his father, Cronos, before establishing his rule on Mount Olympus. His wife, Hera, goddess of marriage, was jealous because of his many love affairs, during which he fathered the gods Apollo and Artemis, and the heroes Perseus and Heracles (or Hercules).

THE RAINMAKER
The Canaanite storm god Baal made thunder with his mace and produced lightning from his lance. Baal revolted against El, his father, by defeating El's favorite, Yam, the god of the sea. Another myth tells of his long battle against Mot, god of death.

The feathers of more than 250 quetzal birds make up this headdress

BABYLONIAN KING OF THE GODS
This doglike dragon is the symbol of Marduk, the Babylonian king of the gods. Strong and heroic, he was given authority over the other gods, including his father, Ea, the god of wisdom, when he agreed to slay the dragon Tiamat (one of two primal beings). Marduk created humankind from the blood of Tiamat's son Kingu.

Aztec serpent god Quetzalcoatl

FEATHERED SERPENT
Half-snake, half-bird, Quetzalcoatl was the Aztec lord of life and god of the winds. He descended to the underworld to retrieve the bones of early humans in order to create new beings. The underworld was ruled by his father, the death god Mictlantecuhtli.

Headdress of Montezuma II, the last Aztec ruler

Wooden kantele from Karelia in Finland, 1893

Stoneware Taoist shrine of the Ming dynasty, 1406 A.D.

Lao-tzu, the founder of Taoism, is shown riding a buffalo

SINGING SHAMAN
Vainamoinen, the eternal singer, was the son of the Finnish air-goddess Ilmatar. He was born old, so no one wanted to marry him — one girl, Aino, even became a mermaid rather than be his bride. Vainamoinen was a shaman, whose songs to the sound of his harplike kantele were acts of creative magic.

The Jade Emperor

LORD OF THE HEAVENS
The Chinese gods formed a huge bureaucracy, at the head of which was the Jade Emperor. He was assisted by the God of the Eastern Peak, who had no fewer than 75 departments under his control, each supervised by lesser gods. The Jade Emperor's wife was Xi Wang Mu, the Queen Mother of the West, guardian of the peaches of immortality, which she serves at a great feast once every 1,000 years.

Ebony mortar and pestle from Tanzania, East Africa

Mortar

Pestle

The God of the Eastern Peak

STAIRWAY TO HEAVEN
Nyame is the sky god of the Ashanti of Africa. He used to live close to humans, but when an old woman annoyed him by knocking him with her pestle as she pounded yams, he moved away toward the heavens. The old woman and her sons tried to reach him by piling mortars on top of each other, but they were one short. They took the mortar from the bottom to place it on the top, and the pile collapsed, killing them all.

19

Floods and storms

THE STORY OF A GREAT FLOOD that once overwhelmed the Earth – a flood that only a lucky few survived – is one of the most widespread of all myths. The earliest flood story is found in the Mesopotamian epic of Gilgamesh, in which Utnapishtim frees birds to see if the waters are subsiding. The Native American Mandan tribe spoke of Lone Man, who survived a great flood in his big canoe. The Greek god Zeus, tired of the wickedness of humans, sent a flood to drown them all. But the giant Prometheus warned his son Deucalion, who built an ark in time to save himself and his wife.

SAVED BY A FISH
One day the Hindu sage Manu found a fish in his washing water. The fish told Manu that he should build a ship because a great flood was coming. When the flood arrived, the fish, which was an incarnation of the Hindu god Vishnu, towed Manu to safety. Manu then became the father of all humankind.

Giant Wave, a print of a tsunami (huge, violent wave) by Katsushika Hokusai (1760–1849)

A tsunami is usually caused by an earthquake or a volcano; here, a tsunami batters a Japanese plank boat

KINGDOM OF ATLANTIS
Poseidon, the Greek god of the sea, fell in love with a woman called Clito and built her a paradise island. Clito bore Poseidon sons, who founded the kingdom of Atlantis on the island. The brothers ruled the island in wisdom. But later rulers became greedy and corrupt, so Poseidon sent a tidal wave to swallow up Atlantis and all its people.

MAYAN RAINMAKER
Chac, the rain god, broke open a great rock to uncover the first corn plant. And it was Chac who sent the rain each year to enable the corn to grow. But sometimes, instead of gentle rain, Chac sent violent storms, in which he wielded his weapon, lightning.

In his left hand, Chac carries a bowl; in his right, a ball of smoking incense

Headdress of tropical bird feathers

Type of poncho worn by Sapa Incas, the first of whom named himself after the supreme god Viracocha

GIANT WAVES
The great flood is caused either by a deluge of rain, as in the Noah story (below), or by a gigantic tidal wave that sweeps over the land, as in the story of Atlantis (above). Both are terrifying images of unstoppable destruction.

CREATOR OF HUMANS
Viracocha, the Inca creator god, was displeased with his first attempt at creating humans from stone, so he drowned them all in a flood. He then tried again, this time making the people from clay. He wandered among these new people as a beggar, teaching them how to live.

NOAH AND THE ARK
When God saw how wicked humans had become, he decided to drown them all, for he was sorry he had ever created them. But he decided to save one good man, Noah. He warned Noah to build an ark in which to save his family and two of every living creature to people the Earth after the great flood. When the flooding subsided, God set the rainbow in the sky as a promise that he would never again destroy humanity by a flood.

Some believe that gods live at the peak of Mount Fuji in Japan, which is always capped with snow

The elements

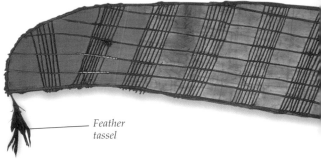

ALL OVER the world, the elemental forces that form it have been the focus of myth-making. Fire, air, earth, and water are the "four elements" in Western tradition. The Chinese have five elements: wood, fire, earth, metal, and water. Almost all mythologies tell how humans acquired the gift of fire, often stolen from the sun. Gods of the air and the sky have been so important that the names of many supreme gods, such as the Greek Zeus, simply mean "sky." The Earth, though sometimes regarded as male, is more often thought of as our mother. According to the mythology of ancient Babylon, in the beginning nothing existed but Apsu, the freshwater ocean; and Tiamat, the saltwater ocean. These two waters have given and taken life since the dawn of time.

Feather tassel

Agni's stomach is full because fire devours everything

FIRE-EATER
Wherever a fire is lit, the Hindu fire god Agni is born. Because he is present in all homes, he knows all secrets. He once helped a man find his wife, who had been carried away by the sage Bhrigu. Bhrigu then cursed Agni, making him consume all the dirt of the Earth. But as Agni devours the dirt, he also purifies it with his flames.

VOLCANIC PELE
In Hawaii, which is dominated by the Kilauea volcano, Pele is worshiped as the goddess of fire. She is as passionate and dangerous as a volcano. She fell in love with the prince of Kauai, but when he preferred her sister, she encased him in molten lava and turned him to stone.

OCEANS OF OLOKUN
Olokun, the sea king of the Edo people of Benin, Nigeria, is a powerful god. He is the source of all wealth and the bringer of children, whose souls must cross the ocean to be born. His palace is a paradise, full of the noise of children, and his wives, who are the rivers. The Olokun river is the source of all the waters of the Earth, including the ocean.

Mother-of-pearl eyes embedded in a painted face

Kite is made of canvas and twigs

SKY MAN
Tawhaki, the great Polynesian hero whom the Maori call the god of thunder and lightning, ascended to the sky world as a kite, seeking to avenge his father, Hema, whose eyes had been gouged out by goblins to use as lights. Maori priests foretold the future by watching the dance of kites in the air.

Maori kite in the form of a bird with a human head

Balls of rolling thunder

The thunder god is depicted as a demon in the air

Drumstick makes the thunder

EARTH MOTHER
Toci, mother of the gods, was an important Aztec earth goddess. She was a goddess of the harvest, of childbirth, and of curing, but also of war and discord. The Earth itself was said to have been made by the gods from the body of the fearsome goddess Tlaltecuhtli, who could be appeased only by being given human hearts to eat.

Aztec earth goddess (A.D. 1300–1521)

Poseidon's trident, a three-pronged fisherman's spear

Aboriginal stone ax from Northern Territory, Australia

THUNDER ROLLS
This burly Japanese god (possibly Kami-Nari, the god of rolling thunder) beats out thunder on his drum. Japanese thunder deities are threatening forces. When Izanagi, the primal male, descended to hell in search of his wife, the decomposing goddess sent eight thunder gods to chase him from the underworld.

LIGHTNING MAN
The Lightning Brothers are important ancestor figures in the Dreamtime of the Aborigines of Australia's Northern Territory. Tcabuinji killed his younger brother, Wagtjadbulla, with a stone ax in an argument about Tcabuinji's wife. It is this ax that Tcabuinji uses to split trees when lightning strikes.

STORMY SEAS
Poseidon, the Greek god of the sea, had a violent and vengeful nature. This showed in his persecution of the hero Odysseus, who had blinded the god's son. As well as causing storms at sea, Poseidon was also believed to cause earthquakes.

Japanese thunder god

The natural world

ALL THE ELEMENTS OF THE NATURAL WORLD — animals, flowers, plants, and trees — are the gifts of the gods and remain in their care. Many cultures worshiped the Earth as a mother goddess, provider of food and fertility. But they also gave responsibility for important crops — such as maize for Native Americans, or rice for the Japanese — to specific gods or goddesses. Hunting societies believe that game is withheld or released by divinities such as Sedna, the North American Inuit mistress of the sea beasts. In the forests of northern Cameroon, hunters pray to the Bedimo, ancestral spirits, to release game from their divine stables.

Spanish reed

This type of reed has been used to make pipes for 5,000 years

Cobs of corn

PAN'S PIPES
With his goatlike horns and legs, Pan was the Greek god of the pastures, especially of sheep and goats. He could inspire fear in his enemies, who would flee in what we now call a "panic." Pan was also very amorous. One nymph, Syrinx, turned into reeds to escape him. But Pan made himself a set of musical pipes from the reeds so that she would always be close to him.

SPRINGTIME GOD
The Aztec god of spring, Xipec Totec, allowed his skin to be flayed (peeled off) in order to promote new growth from within — like a corn seed breaking through its husk to become a new plant. At festivals in his honor, young men wore the skins of human sacrificial offerings.

Farmers harvesting rice

RICE SUPPLIES
Every village in Japan has a shrine dedicated to the rice god Inari, who comes down from his mountain home in the spring and returns in the autumn, after the rice harvest.

Rice grains

Wooden mask representing
the nature spirits of the
North American Inuits

Kelp
seaweed

MOTHER OF SEA BEASTS
Sedna, the Inuit sea woman,
was thrown into the sea by
her father because she married
a dog. When she tried to cling
to the kayak (boat), he chopped
off her fingers, which turned
into the first sea mammals. To
show her appreciation for the
help given her by humans,
who comb her hair, Sedna
releases the sea beasts so
that humankind can feed.

*Mask represents the various sea
beasts, such as seals and fish,
that Sedna watches over*

*This Maori ceremonial
adze (axlike tool)
symbolizes Tane, who
was himself shaped by
craftsmen with adzes*

TANE OF THE TREES
The Oceanic forest god Tane
lived in the highest heaven,
from which he brought down
three baskets of knowledge for
humankind. He made himself a
wife, Hine-hau-one (the Earth-
formed maiden), from red
sand. Their daughter, the
dawn maiden, ran away to
become Hine-nui-te-Po,
the goddess of death.

*Flora awakens
the flowers
with her
sweet music*

FLOWERING FLORA
Flora was the Roman goddess of the
flowers, who made plants and trees
bloom. Flora also had a flower which
made women pregnant when they
touched it. She lent the flower to the
goddess Juno, who soon became
pregnant with Mars, the god of war.

Celtic bronze horse found in the tomb of a prince (c. 5th century B.C.)

EQUESTRIAN EPONA
Epona, the Celtic horse goddess, is closely linked to the triple mother goddesses, who are often shown nursing babies. Like them, Epona is often shown with wheat and other fertility symbols, but she was especially associated with horse breeding. Horse breeding was crucial because the Celts farmed with horses, and without them could not have grown enough food.

Fertility and birth

WORSHIP OF THE GREAT MOTHER goddess, often identified as the Earth, has been part of many religions since the dawn of humanity. For instance, Pacha Mama, the name of the Inca fertility goddess, means "earth mother." When the Hittite god of farming, Telepinu, withdrew from the world in a rage, and humans began to starve, it was the mother goddess Hannahanna who found him. The myth of the Greek corn goddess Demeter and her despairing search for her lost daughter Persephone, during which the Earth became a wasteland, was at the heart of Greek religion. Birth and fertility were not exclusively the reserve of goddesses. Frey was the Norse god of fertility, a role given in Egypt to the gods Min and Osiris; Egyptian mothers wanted the aid of the impish god Bes at childbirth.

FREY AND FREYA
Twin brother and sister Frey and Freya were Norse fertility gods. Frey's cult involved his image being carried from place to place in a wagon during the winter months to ensure fertility. Freya, who was considered to be the most beautiful of all goddesses, was primarily the goddess of love and of soothsaying (predicting the future).

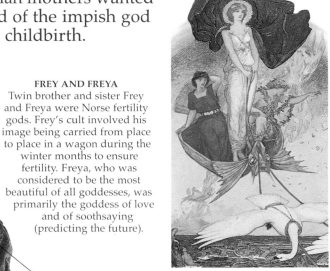

Goddess Freya in her chariot

Frey holds his beard, a symbol of growth, in one hand

JADE SKIRT
Chalchiuhtlicue, "she of the jade skirt," was the central Mexican goddess of lakes and streams and, by association, the goddess of birth. She is sometimes depicted with a pair of babies, one male and one female. Chalchiuhtlicue once flooded the Earth but turned humankind into fish so that they were saved.

The water goddess Chalchiutlicue stands in water near a giant centipede

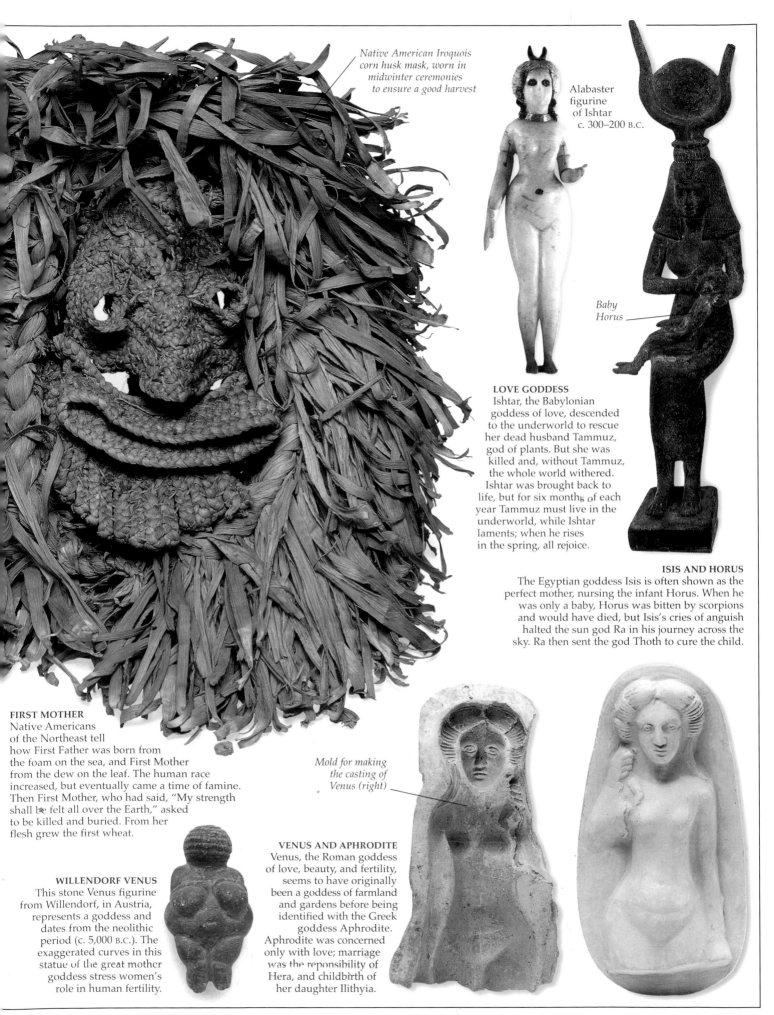

Native American Iroquois corn husk mask, worn in midwinter ceremonies to ensure a good harvest

Alabaster figurine of Ishtar c. 300–200 B.C.

Baby Horus

LOVE GODDESS
Ishtar, the Babylonian goddess of love, descended to the underworld to rescue her dead husband Tammuz, god of plants. But she was killed and, without Tammuz, the whole world withered. Ishtar was brought back to life, but for six months of each year Tammuz must live in the underworld, while Ishtar laments; when he rises in the spring, all rejoice.

ISIS AND HORUS
The Egyptian goddess Isis is often shown as the perfect mother, nursing the infant Horus. When he was only a baby, Horus was bitten by scorpions and would have died, but Isis's cries of anguish halted the sun god Ra in his journey across the sky. Ra then sent the god Thoth to cure the child.

FIRST MOTHER
Native Americans of the Northeast tell how First Father was born from the foam on the sea, and First Mother from the dew on the leaf. The human race increased, but eventually came a time of famine. Then First Mother, who had said, "My strength shall be felt all over the Earth," asked to be killed and buried. From her flesh grew the first wheat.

Mold for making the casting of Venus (right)

WILLENDORF VENUS
This stone Venus figurine from Willendorf, in Austria, represents a goddess and dates from the neolithic period (c. 5,000 B.C.). The exaggerated curves in this statue of the great mother goddess stress women's role in human fertility.

VENUS AND APHRODITE
Venus, the Roman goddess of love, beauty, and fertility, seems to have originally been a goddess of farmland and gardens before being identified with the Greek goddess Aphrodite. Aphrodite was concerned only with love; marriage was the reponsibility of Hera, and childbirth of her daughter Ilithyia.

Children of the gods

IN MANY MYTHOLOGIES, THE GODS reproduce just as human beings do. Their children may be other gods (who may even take over from them), or semidivine heroes, such as Cuchulain and Hercules. Some supreme deities, such as the Norse god Odin and the Greek god Zeus, are called "all-father" in recognition of the role they play for other beings. However, not all children of the gods are beneficial to the world. For instance, the Norse god Loki gave birth to the fierce wolf Fenrir and Hel, the mistress of the underworld; the Greek god of the sea, Poseidon, fathered the brutal Cyclops Polyphemus. Gods can also incarnate themselves in human or animal form, as the Hindu god Vishnu does in his various guises, such as Narasimba, the half-man, half-lion; and Vamana, the dwarf.

Matsya, the fish

Kurma, the turtle

Varaha, the boar

INCARNATIONS OF VISHNU
The Hindu god Vishnu, the preserver, has been incarnated nine times in different forms. As the fish, Vishnu saved Manu, the first man, from the great flood. As the turtle, he helped the gods churn the ocean and win the elixir of immortality. Vishnu raised the Earth out of the sea as Varaha the boar. And as the hero Rama, he rescued his wife from a demon. Vishnu's tenth avatar, Kalki, the horse, will come to destroy and re-create the world at the end of this cycle of time.

Cuchulain rides his chariot into battle

FATHER OF THE PHARAOHS
Falcon-headed Horus, whose eyes were the sun and the moon, was the child of the Egyptian gods Isis and Osiris. He was conceived when Isis breathed life into the mummified Osiris, who had been murdered by his brother Seth. The long battle between Horus and Seth was vicious, but eventually Horus prevailed. The Egyptian pharaohs traced their descent from him and were called the "living Horus."

UGLY WARRIOR
Cuchulain, a hero of Irish mythology, was a fierce warrior. His father was the sun god Lugh. Although normally very handsome, on the battlefield Cuchulain became a monster. One eye disappeared into his head, the other bulged; his heels turned to the front; and his jaws opened wide enough to swallow an enemy's head. Before he was killed, Cuchulain strapped himself to a standing stone so that he would die standing up.

Prince Rama

THE WATER TWINS
The Dogon people of Mali in West Africa say that the creator spirit Amma first mated with the Earth, and the Nommo (water) twins were born. Human on the top half and snakelike on the bottom half, the twins were made out of the life-force of Amma. The Nommo were green in color, and clothed their mother Earth with plants and trees. They are believed to make an outline of every newborn soul, giving it a twin nature, both male and female.

HEROIC HERACLES
The Greek hero Heracles (Hercules in Latin) was the son of Zeus by a mortal woman, Alcmene. As an infant he proved his divine descent by strangling two deadly serpents sent by Zeus's jealous wife Hera. Hera's hatred pursued Heracles all his life, robbing him of his destined throne.

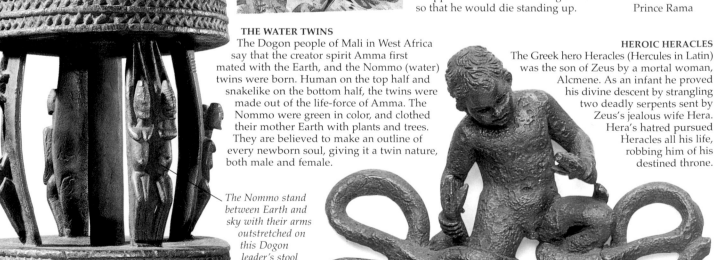

The Nommo stand between Earth and sky with their arms outstretched on this Dogon leader's stool

28

Scary monsters

Giants are found throughout mythology. Their size makes them terrifying, but often they are portrayed as slow, stupid, and easily outwitted, like the Cyclops Polyphemus, who believes that the hero Odysseus's name is Nobody and yells out "Nobody is hurting me" when Odysseus blinds him. Many of the first beings were monsters, such as Ymir, the Norse frost giant.

Cyclopes had only one eye

Fierce incisors tear meat from the bone

ONE-EYED OGRE
Polyphemus was one of the legendary Cyclopes, one-eyed giants with ferocious appetites. He was blinded by Odysseus, who plunged a red-hot stake into his eye. But Polyphemus's father, Poseidon, was so enraged that he persecuted Odysseus — wrecking his ships, drowning his crews, and keeping him from his home for ten long years.

Skulls of mastodons (extinct elephant-like mammals) were once believed to be Cyclopes' skulls

Greedy Cyclopes could devour whole carcasses at one sitting

Tunic made from the hides of the Cyclops's prey

Cyclopes tore their prey limb from limb

29

Ancestor worship

IN MANY CULTURES, FEAR OF THE EVIL POWER of spirits of the dead is balanced by a belief in the protective power of the spirits of ancestors, who are believed to watch over and guide the living. For this reason offerings may be made to ancestors' shrines. For instance, in China the head of a family must make regular sacrifices of food at the graves of his ancestors; if not, the "hungry ghosts" may cause trouble. In both China and Japan, wooden tablets inscribed with the names of ancestors are kept in a household shrine. The duty that the living owe to the dead was never more pressing than in ancient Egypt, where it was vital that the eldest living son of deceased parents raise a monument to their memory and pronounce their names every time he passed it, to keep their names alive.

ROMULUS AND REMUS
Romulus was the mythical founder of Rome; his name means simply "Roman." The twins Romulus and Remus were the sons of the war god Mars. Abandoned as babies, they were suckled by a wolf and raised by a shepherd. The brothers argued about who should found Rome, and Romulus killed Remus with a spade. But Romulus was soon swept off to heaven by his father, where he became a god and was worshiped by the citizens of Rome.

Bronze figurine group from Benin in Yoruba, West Africa

Female figure from Middle Sepik River, Papua New Guinea

Procession of Oshun's devotees

OSHUN WORSHIP
Ancestors are worshiped in many parts of Africa and are prayed to for good health, fertility, and good fortune. The Yoruba people of West Africa worship Oshun, goddess of the river that bears the same name. Oshun was married to the thunder god Shango and has human descendants. People bathe in the Oshun River to protect themselves from disease. Women, in particular, consult the goddess Oshun in cases of family problems or illness.

LIFE-GIVING ANCESTORS
In New Guinea, carved figures of ancestors were present at *moguru* (life-giving ceremonies) at which the young were initiated into adulthood and the men gained prowess as fighters. In the Papuan Gulf, the fierce Kerua headhunters hung human skulls from carved boards as offerings to ancestral beings.

30

COLOSSAL CHIEFS
On Easter Island, a remote and barren island of volcanic rock stranded in the eastern Pacific, stand hundreds of monolithic stone figures. They are *moai* — figures of dead chiefs who were regarded as descendants of the gods.

FEAST OF LANTERNS
The *bon* festival, held in Japan each July, is known as the Feast of Lanterns. It is held in honor of the spirits of the dead, which return to Earth for the three days of the festival. Relatives of the deceased pray at shrines, where they leave food and other treats for the spirits to feast on.

Papuan ancestral tablets, or ceremonial boards

DREAMTIME ANCESTORS
The Dreamtime is the eternal present in which the revered ancestors of the Australian Aborigines exist, constantly creating the world. Creation story designs, shown to the Aborigines by the ancestors, are still painted on bodies, rocks, and bark, as in the painting (left) from Arnhem Land, North Australia. Aborigines carve pictures showing events in the Dreamtime on sacred wooden and stone artifacts, called *churinga*. These objects embody ancestral spiritual power and must not be seen by women or the uninitiated.

Aboriginal stone knife similar to those used by the eternal ancestors to create humans

Bark sheath

Evil forces

BESIDES GODS OF DEATH and sterility, there are many demons and forces of evil in world mythology. Balanced against these are forces of good which came into being to rid the world of evil. In Siberia it is told how the creator Ulgan made himself a companion, Erlik, from mud floating on the primal ocean. But Erlik, jealous of Ulgan, saved mud to try to build his own world, and he breathed life into humankind without Ulgan's permission. For these betrayals, Erlik was banished to the underworld, where he sits surrounded by evil spirits. Evil beings are very active in Hindu mythology, which has many antigods and demons. One of the most fearsome of all evil spirits is Vucub-Caquix, the Mayan monster macaw who claimed to be both the sun and the moon. He was killed in a terrible battle by the hero twins Hunahpu and Xbalanque, though not before he had torn off Hunahpu's arm.

Gap-toothed Louhi as an eagle-woman with scythe-like claws

WICKED LOUHI
The Finnish hag Louhi promised the smith Ilmarinen her daughter in return for the Sampo — a magic mill that grinds out grain, salt, and money. But Louhi proved treacherous, so Ilmarinen stole back the Sampo and set sail. Louhi turned into a bird and attacked the boat. In the struggle, the Sampo fell to the bottom of the sea, where it still grinds out salt to this day.

Vajrapani holds a thunderbolt in his right hand

Tibetan statue of Vajrapani in his "ferocious" form

Fiery headdress encrusted with turquoise

TREACHEROUS TRICKSTER
Loki, the Norse trickster god, turned against the other gods and brought about the death of Balder the Beautiful, son of the god Odin. For this, he is bound in agony, with poison dripping onto his face, until the final battle of Ragnarok, when he will lead an army from Hel against the gods in a ship made from dead men's nails.

DESTROYER OF EVIL
The Tibetan Vajrapani destroys the wicked with his *vajra* (thunderbolt), which spits lightning. One of eight main bodhisattvas, or Buddhist saints, Vajrapani shares characteristics with Indra, the Hindu god of the skies.

Vajrapani, wielder of the thunderbolt, is a symbol of law and order

Baba Yaga uses her pestle to stir up storms and spread disease

CANNIBAL WITCH
Baba Yaga is the cannibal witch of Russian myth. She lives in a revolving hut supported by hen's feet, and travels through the air in a mortar. Her male equivalent is Koshchei the Deathless, who abducts maidens and can turn into a dragon.

SULKY SUSANO
While bathing, the Japanese god Izanagi gave birth to three powerful divinities: the sun goddess Amaterasu, moon god Tsuki-Yomi, and Susano, the god of storms and chaos. Susano was meant to rule the sea, but he threw a tantrum and said he would rather go to the underworld. He flung a skinned horse into Amaterasu's sacred weaving hall, so was banished to Earth. There he rescued Kusa-nada-hime, the Rice Paddy Princess, from an eight-headed dragon, and made her his wife.

Text from a 19th-century print of the storm god Susano and his wife

Rice Paddy
Princess Kusa-nada-hime

FIRST HUMAN SACRIFICE
When the Aztec goddess Coatlicue was pregnant with the supreme god Huitzilopochtli, she was attacked and murdered by her jealous daughter, Coyolxauhqui, and Coyolxauhqui's 400 brothers. But Huitzilopochtli leaped fully formed from his mother's decapitated body and slew his sister, making her the first human sacrifice.

Each of Durga's ten hands holds a special weapon — a symbol of divine power

INVINCIBLE DURGA
The Hindu warrior goddess Durga was one of the guises of the great goddess Devi. Durga was created to fight the *asuras* (demon enemies of the gods), who had conquered heaven. In each of her ten hands Durga holds a special weapon that she used to cut off the head of the buffalo-king of the *asuras*.

Susano, the
Japanese storm god

BRAVE ANTIGONE
Antigone was the daughter of Oedipus, king of Thebes in Greece. After his death, his two sons, Eteocles and Polynices, fought over the throne and killed each other. Their uncle Creon buried Eteocles with honor but threw the body of Polynices out to rot, regarding him as a traitor. Although threatened with death, Antigone bravely defied her uncle and gave Polynices a token burial, sprinkling three handfuls of dust over the corpse. Creon then walled her up in a cave without food or water, so she hanged herself.

Polynices's corpse is left to rot

Superheroes

MEN AND WOMEN WHO PERFORM great feats of daring and courage are celebrated in all mythologies. Often, they are said to be the children of gods or to be specially favored by the gods. Some heroes can defeat a whole series of enemies in single combat and rid countries of the monsters that plague them. Others, such as Hiawatha, are celebrated as peacemakers rather than as warriors. A typical hero is the Tibetan Gesar, who was a god chosen to be born as a man to rid the world of demons. Gesar became a powerful warrior king, with an immortal horse that flew through the sky and spoke all languages. At the end of his life, Gesar retired to heaven, but one day he will return, for evil can never be wholly defeated.

When Krishna plays his magic flute, women within earshot join him to dance

Krishna is always blue, which shows that he is an incarnation of Vishnu

Krishna is supported by a bed of lotus flowers

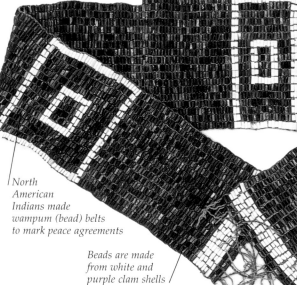

North American Indians made wampum (bead) belts to mark peace agreements

Beads are made from white and purple clam shells

DEMON DODGER
Krishna is the eighth avatar (incarnation) of the Hindu god Vishnu and is worshiped as a god in his own right. When he was a child, his mother took him to the countryside to escape the demon king Kansa, who was persecuting them. Kansa sent a female demon to poison him, but Krishna sucked the life out of her instead.

PEACEMAKER
Dekanah-wida was born to bring tidings of peace from the chief of the Sky Spirits to five warring Native American Indian tribes. Dekanah-wida made the Mohawk chief, Hiawatha, his peacemaker. Hiawatha then traveled between the tribes, persuading them to form the Iroquois League, whose members swore to live in peace together.

Sigurd kills the dragon

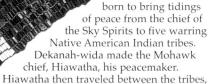

Fafnir the dragon

DRAGON SLAYER
The Scandinavian hero Sigurd slew the dragon Fafnir so that he could claim its treasure. Sigurd had been urged to kill the dragon by Regin, Fafnir's brother, who asked Sigurd to return with the dragon's heart. But Regin was plotting to kill Sigurd and steal the treasure for himself. Some birds tried to warn Sigurd, but he could not understand them. Fortunately, as he cooked the dragon's heart he burned his thumb and, putting it in his mouth, tasted the dragon's blood. The blood enabled Sigurd to understand the birds. Learning that Regin meant to betray him, Sigurd killed him and kept the treasure.

When Yi shot the suns, they fell to the Earth in the shape of crows

The Minotaur had a bull's head on a man's body

MONSTER KILLER
Theseus was the greatest of all Athenian heroes, said to be the son of the sea god Poseidon. His most famous feat was to slay the ferocious Minotaur. King Minos of Crete regularly fed the Minotaur with children from Athens; Theseus volunteered himself to be fed to the Minotaur and, with the help of Minos's daughter Ariadne, killed the Minotaur in the labyrinth (maze) in which he lived.

Yi won a potion of immortality, but Chang E drank it herself and floated to the moon

Heavenly gates are guarded by two soldiers

Mortals on their way to heaven to become immortals

YI THE ARCHER
The Chinese say that originally there were ten suns, the sons of the emperor of the eastern heavens. The suns took turns lighting the sky. But once, all ten went out to play. Together they were so hot that they began to scorch the Earth, so the emperor sent Yi, the heavenly archer, to teach them a lesson. Yi shot down nine of them. The emperor was so upset that he stripped Yi and his wife, Chang E, of their immortality and banished them from heaven.

Perseus holds Medusa's severed head

GREEK GUARDIAN
Perseus was the son of the Greek god Zeus and the maiden Danaë. To save his mother from an unwanted marriage, Perseus agreed to fetch the head of the Gorgon Medusa, whose glance turned the onlooker to stone. Using a bronze shield as a mirror so that he did not have to meet the Gorgon's gaze, Perseus cut off her head. He then used the head to turn his mother's unwelcome suitor to stone.

Kneeling men and women mourn for the dead

Altars full of food

Gilgamesh clutches a captured lion cub

KING GILGAMESH
Gilgamesh was the great hero of ancient Mesopotamia. He was a semidivine king, who fought monsters with his friend Enkidu. When Gilgamesh scorned the love of the goddess Ishtar, she sent a great bull to destroy him, but Gilgamesh and Enkidu slew the bull.

Scenes of the afterlife

Chinese funeral banner, 2nd century B.C.

Medusa lies dead at Perseus's feet

Divine weapons

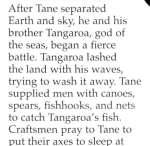

SWORD, SPEAR, AX, AND BOW — the weapons of the gods often mirror those of humans. The Norse all-father Odin, for instance, had a magical spear that he used to stir up war. But the gods can also unleash natural forces as weapons, most notably the thunderbolt (lightning), which has been a weapon of sky gods all over the world. Weapons could be improvised out of anything: the club of the semidivine Greek hero Heracles was simply an uprooted olive tree. The Navajo hero twins were given bows with arrows of lightning by their father, the sun god, to help them rid the world of monsters. Even when caught without their weapons, gods can punish the insolent or wicked. When the Greek hunter Actaeon spied the goddess Diana bathing, without her bow and arrows, she turned him into a stag and let his own hounds maul him to death.

The Greek god Zeus wields a thunderbolt

BATTLING BROTHERS
This 19th-century chief's ax is a symbol of Tane, the Oceanic god of the forests, who was himself shaped by craftsmen with axes. After Tane separated Earth and sky, he and his brother Tangaroa, god of the seas, began a fierce battle. Tangaroa lashed the land with his waves, trying to wash it away. Tane supplied men with canoes, spears, fishhooks, and nets to catch Tangaroa's fish. Craftsmen pray to Tane to put their axes to sleep at night, and to wake them up in the morning.

Shango looks both ways, so that no one can escape him

SPITTER OF THUNDERBOLTS
Ceremonial staffs such as this symbolize Shango, thunder god of the Yoruba people of West Africa. His symbol is the double ax, which represents thunderbolts. Shango was originally a king and was given the power to spit thunderbolts by the trickster god Eshu. Being hit by lightning is thought to be a sign of Shango's anger.

To terrify Shango's enemies, his devotees hold thunderbolt staffs as they dance to loud drumbeats

THUNDER AND LIGHTNING
The terrifying energy of an electrical storm has been interpreted by many people as the anger of the gods. Thunderbolts have been used as weapons by many gods, including the Olympian Zeus. Native Americans revere the Thunderbird, which produces thunder by flapping its wings and lightning by flashing its eyes. Tupan, an Amazonian thunder god, caused thunder and lightning by crossing the sky in a wooden trough.

MAGICAL SWORD
The Norse god Frey had a sword that would fight on its own. But he gave the sword to Skirnir, his servant, as a reward for winning him the hand of the beautiful maiden Gerd. It is said that at the final battle of Ragnarok, Frey will fight the fire giant Surt, who has a blade that flames like the sun. But without his sword, Frey will be defeated, allowing Surt to burn up the world.

Iron sword from Denmark

ANCESTRAL WEAPON
The boomerang was an important weapon of the Australian Aborigines. The first boomerang represented the Aboriginal Rainbow Snake, and is said to have been made from the tree between heaven and Earth. A myth of the Binbinga tribe of Australia tells how the ancestral snake Bobbi-Bobbi made the first boomerang from one of his ribs.

Rainbow Snake

Aboriginal war boomerangs are designed to fly in straight lines and travel great distances

17th-century brass *vajras* from Tibet representing thunderbolts

Tibetans use vajras, *believed to hold magical powers, in rituals and while meditating*

BLADE OF IRON
Ogun is the god of iron and war among the Yoruba people of West Africa. When the Earth was still a watery waste, Ogun used to climb down from heaven on a spider's web to hunt in the marshland. After the Earth was formed, Ogun cleared the land with his iron blade. He was last seen sinking into the ground with his sword.

Ritual sword used in Ogun worship

Vows taken in the name of Ogun, with the tongue on a blade or some other iron object, are completely binding

Ceremonial bow and arrows

GODDESS OF HUNTING
Diana is the Roman name for the Greek goddess of hunting and archery, Artemis. Although Diana was the goddess of the hunt, she was also the protector of all wild animals.

Diana, protector of wild animals

Silver replica of Thor's hammer from Denmark

Thor in his chariot pulled by goats

THOR'S LUCKY HAMMER
The Norse thunder god Thor was the son of the all-father Odin; his mother was the Earth. He had a wonderful hammer, *Mjollnir*, which never missed its target, and returned to his hand when thrown. Vikings wore pendants in the shape of Thor's hammer for protection. Large replicas of these lucky hammers were also used to bless weddings, births, and funerals.

Gods of war

Hᴜᴍᴀɴ ʜɪsᴛᴏʀʏ ʜᴀs ʙᴇᴇɴ sʜᴀᴘᴇᴅ by war and conflict, and gods of war have a high status in many mythologies. The Greeks had two war gods: Ares, who was the god of fighting; and Athena, who was the goddess of strategy. That a goddess should take an interest in warfare is not unusual. Ishtar was the Mesopotamian goddess of both love and war; the Irish had a triple war goddess, the Morrigan, who could change into a crow and settled in that form on the shoulder of the dying hero Cuchulain. But most war gods are male, and many of them, like Ares and Odin, are bloodthirsty, reveling in slaughter.

GREEK GODDESS OF STRATEGY
While Ares was the Greek god of fighting, Athena was the goddess of strategy and wisdom. She sprang from the head of her father Zeus, fully armed and ready for battle. Athena is always depicted in full armor, with the head of the Gorgon Medusa fixed to her breastplate.

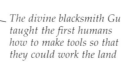

The divine blacksmith Gu taught the first humans how to make tools so that they could work the land

Mars wears a warrior's helmet

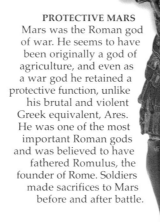

PROTECTIVE MARS
Mars was the Roman god of war. He seems to have been originally a god of agriculture, and even as a war god he retained a protective function, unlike his brutal and violent Greek equivalent, Ares. He was one of the most important Roman gods and was believed to have fathered Romulus, the founder of Rome. Soldiers made sacrifices to Mars before and after battle.

GOD OF IRON
Gu was the fifth-born child of Mawu-Lisa, the West African creator god. Mawu gave her strength to Gu. He is made of iron and is sometimes depicted as an iron sword. In this form, Mawu-Lisa used him to clear the Earth for humans to live in. Gu is the god of iron and consequently of war, since war is waged with iron weapons.

Iron statue of Gu, war god of the Fon people of West Africa

WARRING KU
Ku was the war god of Hawaii. He had many names descriptive of his various roles. As patron of woodworkers he was Ku-adzing-out-the-canoe. When the gods were trapped between their parents Earth and sky, Ku-of-the-angry-face wanted to kill them, but the other gods fought Ku. This was the beginning of warfare.

Valkyries rode horses to fetch dead warriors from the battlefield and take them to Odin's Valhalla

FIGHTING SPIRITS
The Valkyries of the Norse god Odin were female spirits who rode to battle to give victory or death, according to Odin's will. They also waited on the souls of dead warriors in the hall of Valhalla. The name Valkyrie means "chooser of the slain." The Norse fertility goddess Freya was said to ride to battle and claim half the slain.

All-father Odin wears an elaborate winged helmet

Chinese bronze sword, 4th century B.C.

NORSE WAR GODS
The Viking gods were among the most warlike of all. Their leader, Odin (left), was the god of battle, inspiring his warriors with a fighting frenzy. Only those who died in battle joined him in Valhalla after death.

Spears were among Norse warriors' most prized possessions

DEMON KILLER
Skanda, the six-headed Hindu god of war, is the son of Shiva. He was born to kill the demon Taraka, who had been oppressing the gods. Skanda rides a peacock, on which he traveled around the world in a contest of learning with his brother Ganesh. Ganesh, who stayed at home and read, knew more than Skanda when he returned.

CHINESE WARRIOR GOD
Guan Di is the Chinese god of war. Originally a humble seller of bean curd, he devoted himself to study, and he is still regarded as a patron of literature. However, after he killed a magistrate, he had to flee his home and fend for himself. Guan Di became a soldier, one of the three famous Brothers of the Peach Orchard, and, in 1594 A.D., was elevated to the status of god of war.

Statue of Guan Di, the Chinese god of war

Contacting the spirits

ANCIENT GREEKS TOOK THEIR PROBLEMS to the oracle of Apollo at Delphi, where a priestess, called the pythoness, went into a trance and uttered strange words that were then interpreted by a priest. Among the Vikings, *volvas* (prophetesses), answered questions in a similar way. Siberian shamans, Native American medicine men, and Aboriginal men of high degree all use drumming, dance, and song to enter an altered mental state in which they can communicate with the spirit world. Offerings and sacrifices may also bridge the gap between the two worlds, as when worshipers are possessed by the gods in voodoo rites. Among the Yoruba of West Africa, the god of fate, Eshu, uses sacrifices to plead with the other gods, or to appease evil spirits on behalf of humanity.

GUIDING GOD
The Greek god Hermes (Mercury in Rome) was the messenger of the gods, and also the guide of souls into the underworld. As he was always going to and fro, he became the protector of all travelers.

Pipe of carved human bone

Priest speaks into this hole to distort his voice and make it boom out

VOICE DISGUISER
A priest of the Tiv people of Nigeria would use this voice disguiser to allow the ancestor god Tiv to speak through him in a piercing cry.

Half-halo represents Ganesh's divinity

Noose to trap delusion

CONVEYOR OF PRAYERS
Ganesh, the wise elephant-headed son of Shiva, is the god of all good enterprises. Hindus ask Ganesh to pass on their requests to Shiva. They make offerings to the potbellied god before going on a journey, starting a business, or making plans for a wedding.

Jizo, the protector of children and travelers

GOOD-LUCK CHARMS
Japanese *fuda*, or amulets, bear the name of a god and are used to ward off evil and misfortune and to bring good luck. They are often placed on household shrines to protect the family.

The ancestors sit in the top branches of the world tree; the shaman climbs up to ask for their help

Shamans' spirit helpers often take animal form

Drumbeats are used to call the spirits that will help the shaman

Metal ornaments hanging from the belt protect against evil spirits

THE SHAMAN
A shaman is someone who has had a life-changing vision that enables him or her to enter a trance and fly to the spirit world. A shaman's power is usually used for healing, though it can also cause disease or death.

Souls of the unborn nest in the tree

Dancers hang from rawhide thongs sewn through the skin

SUN DANCE
In rituals such as the sun dance, Plains Native Americans underwent excruciating physical tortures as sacrifices to the Great Spirit. Once they had fulfilled their vows, dancers hoped to receive a vision.

The pipe bowl is round, like the world, and outside it is the endless universe

38457

PIPES OF PEACE
The sacred pipe is an important part of many Native American rituals, bringing peace and healing. Tobacco was believed to have the power to summon good spirits, ward off evil ones, and bring either good luck or bad. Communal smoking helped to reinforce the ties between families, tribes, and the universe.

The world tree houses all souls

Tiger spirits often teach shamans their craft

Spirits

Siberian shaman's outfit

41

Love, fortune, and happiness

MANY PEOPLE WORSHIP deities who will bring them luck in life. In ancient times, for instance, the Romans had a cult of the goddess Fortuna (good luck). The Ewe people of Togo in West Africa believe that the soul of each unborn child must first visit Ngolimeno, the "Mother of the Spirit People." If they please her, she will grant them a happy life. The Japanese worship seven gods of luck, of whom one, Benten, is a goddess. But it is the Chinese who have outdone all others in the worship of fortune and happiness. The lucky Ho-Ho twins (right) are often shown attending Tsai Shen, the god of wealth. Another common trio is Fu Shen, god of happiness; Lu Shen, god of good luck; and Shou Shen, god of longevity.

THE WINGED GOD
Cupid (Eros in Greek) was the mischievous Roman god of love, often shown as a cheeky infant with a bow and arrows. Some of his arrows had gold tips and caused people to fall in love; others were tipped with lead and had the opposite effect.

Venus of Rome rises from the ocean on a scallop shell

BORN OF FOAM
The Greek goddess of love and desire, Aphrodite (Venus to the Romans), was born from the foam of the sea. She devoted herself to pleasure, prided herself on never doing any work, and was often assisted by Eros (Cupid to the Romans). Aphrodite was married to the smith god Hephaestus but had many lovers among both gods and men. As Venus she was the mother of the Roman hero Aeneas.

Each twin carries a jar containing a lotus of purity and perfection

Statue depicting the birth of Aphrodite, Greek goddess of love

Terracotta figure of Aphrodite made in the 2nd century B.C

The gods are standing on beds of lotus flowers

The head of each twin is decorated with a lotus

GOOD FORTUNE GODS

The seven gods of luck (Shichi Fukujin) include Bishamon, Daikoku, Ebisu, Fukurokuju, Hotei, Jorojin, and the goddess Benten – the bringer of love, happiness, and good fortune. The Shichi Fukujin are often shown together on their treasure ship. Their treasures include a hat of invisibility, a lucky rain hat, keys to the divine treasure house, a purse that never empties, a cloak of feathers, rolls of silk, and scrolls or books.

Benten rides an ox, symbol of good fortune

These Ho-Ho gods symbolize happy relations between couples

CONFUSED DEITY

Kwan-non is the god or goddess of mercy in Japanese Buddhism. Priests regard Kwan-non as a male divinity, but most people pray to him as a goddess, and he appears in 33 female forms. This statue shows her (or him) holding a baby. Expectant mothers would pray to this statue as Koyasu Kwan-non ("Kwan-non of easy childbirth").

Love medicines are inserted into pockets on the chest of each doll

LOVE DOLLS

These Native American medicine dolls are used by the Menominee of the western Great Lakes to ensure that a husband and wife remain faithful to each other. The male doll is named after the husband and the female after the wife, and the two are tied together face to face. The Pottawatomi, also of the western Great Lakes, used dolls as charms to make one person fall in love with another.

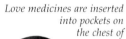

HO-HO TWINS

The two immortals called Ho are the patrons of Chinese merchants. Besides bringing prosperity, they represent harmonious union between couples, because the word "ho" means harmony. Their names were originally Han Shan and Shih-teh. Han Shan was a holy fool who attached himself to the monastery at Kuo-ching Ssu; the monks rejected him, but Shih-teh, an orphan in the kitchens, saved scraps to feed him.

Tricksters

LIGHTHEARTED COMEDY and dark humor are introduced into myths by trickster figures, such as the Native American Coyote (left), whose insatiable curiosity and love of mischief leave havoc and confusion in their wake. Tricksters may be animal, human, or both. Some tricksters hover between good and evil, as does the cunning Norse god Loki. The Ashanti people of West Africa tell tales of Anansi, the cunning spider-man, who won the famous stories of the sky god Nyame. By a series of clever tricks, Anansi trapped all the creatures that Nyame thought were impossible to catch. For instance, he caught the fairy Mmoatia by making a tar baby, to which Mmoatia stuck fast. When Anansi delivered the creatures to Nyame, he was so impressed that he willingly gave Anansi the stories. Since then, the tales have been called spider stories.

WILY COYOTE
Many Native American peoples tell stories of the wily Coyote, who both tricks and is tricked. Coyote has many human characteristics — he is greedy and selfish, and his exploits lead to bad as well as good consequences.

Cowrie shells are used by Eshu to predict the future

MISCHIEVOUS ESHU
Eshu is the trickster god of the Yoruba people of West Africa. His many guises include giant, dwarf, rude boy, wise old man, and a priest, as seen here. Eshu loves mischief. For instance, he broke up a firm friendship between two men by wearing a hat that was white on one side but black on the other, causing them to quarrel about the color of his hat.

Eshu holds a small statue of himself

Mask worn to impersonate Hare

Hare climbs up the mask

CUNNING HARE
Hare is an African animal trickster who became known in America as Brer Rabbit. Cunning and wily, Hare always outwits the other animals, except when Tortoise challenged him to a race. Instead of running, Tortoise placed members of his family all around the course and sat waiting for Hare at the finish line.

Figures represent Eshu in his various guises

An Eshu priest would wear this statue by hooking the headdress over his shoulder, just as Eshu is doing with the statue he is holding

SUN CATCHER
Maui-of-a-thousand-tricks is the trickster hero of Polynesian mythology. He fished up the islands with his magic hook, pushed up the heavens, stole fire for humankind, and snared the sun with his sister's hair to slow it down, so that we have long summer days.

Tengu rescue the hero Tametomo from the jaws of a giant fish

Medicine calabashes (bowls) represent Eshu's magical powers

INVISIBLE TRICKSTERS
The Tengu are Japanese trickster spirits, part-bird, part-man. They are said to be descended from the storm god Susano, who himself got into trouble by playing tricks. Tengu have magic cloaks of invisibility.

GRIMACING GOD
Bes was a popular Egyptian god of music, dance, and laughter, whose grimacing face and comical antics were thought to frighten away evil spirits. He was the protector of mothers in childbirth and the companion of young children. He is always shown sticking his tongue out at the world.

Bacchus's long flowing hair shows his eternal youth

The fish represents the islands that Maui fished up from the sea

INDULGENT GOD
Bacchus (Dionysus in Greek) was the Roman god of wine and ecstasy. His followers were wild women called the Maenads (frenzied ones). When sailors captured Bacchus, his tricks sent them diving madly into the sea, where they turned into dolphins. It was Bacchus who gave King Midas the double-edged gift of turning all that he touched into gold.

Animal idols

GODS AND SPIRITS MAY BE SHOWN in animal form, or as half-human, half-beast. Trickster figures, such as the African spider-man Anansi, may be a man, an animal, or a mixture of both at different times in the same story. Some gods have an animal helper, such as the fox that lived with the Japanese rice god Inari and acted as his messenger. Some gods can transform themselves into animals; the Greek god Zeus, for example, became a bull and then a swan while pursuing his love affairs. Some gods have an animal double, as with the Aztec god Quetzalcoatl and his twin Xolotl — the dog who helped retrieve the bones of humankind from the underworld.

Celtic drinking horns tipped with sheeps' heads

THE HORNED ONE
Gods with animals' horns are found in many mythologies. One of the most famous was the Celtic horned god Cernunnos, who was lord of the beasts, and a god of fertility. The goat's horns of the Greek god Pan inspired pictures of the Christian Devil.

THE BULL OF HEAVEN
This winged bull stood guard over a royal palace in Assyria. The bull was a cult animal all over ancient west Asia. For instance, a bull of heaven was sent to destroy the Sumerian hero Gilgamesh. But Gilgamesh and his friend slew the bull and gave its heart to the sun god Shamash.

Half-human, half-beast

The gods of many peoples are often depicted as half-human, half-animal. This is especially true of the Egyptian gods, nearly all of whom have at least one animal form. For instance, the cow goddess Hathor was also worshipped as the lioness Sekhmet, and the cat Bastet. The dog or jackal god Anubis could also become a snake or a falcon. The sun god Ra turned himself into a cat to cut off the head of the evil snake Apep that attacked him every night.

Nagas have both protective and destructive powers

19th-century Sri Lankan mask

Fierce face wards off the evil spirits thought to cause sickness

THE SNAKE DEMON
This mask of Naga Rassa, or snake demon, is worn in dances to drive away evil spirits. The nagas (sacred snakes) were descended from the ancient sage Kasyapa, the father of life. Buddhists tell how Mucilinda, a king of the nagas, grew more heads to shelter the Buddha from a storm.

SEKHMET
The sun god Ra sent the raging lioness Sekhmet to destroy humankind. But when Ra changed his mind, the only way to stop Sekhmet from killing was to make her drunk.

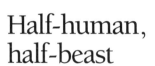

SOBEK
The Egyptian crocodile-god Sobek was unable to resist eating meat, so when the dismembered body of the god Osiris was thrown into the Nile, Sobek gulped some of it down. He was punished for this crime by having his tongue cut out.

ANUBIS
The jackal-headed god Anubis made the first mummy when he wrapped the body parts of the god Osiris in cloth to put them back together. In the underworld, Anubis weighed the hearts of the dead against the feather of justice.

When Garuda soars into the sky, he symbolizes the human spirit

Vishnu and his wife, Lakshmi, ride on Garuda

Golden Garuda's body shines as bright as the sun — some say he was the sun in the form of a bird

Eagle-like wings

Garuda has the body of a human

Legs are covered with golden feathers

KING OF THE BIRDS
Half-human, half-bird, Garuda was the Hindu king of the birds and destroyer of evil. He was ridden by the great god Vishnu. Garuda was the son of Kasyapa (left). But Garuda hated his father's other offspring, the nagas, because their mother made his mother, Vinata, a slave in the underworld. To save her, Garuda had to steal a cup of the elixir of immortality from the gods.

Clawed feet enabled Garuda to pick up the snakes that he devoured

Brass figure of Garuda from Tibet

47

Mythical beasts

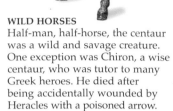

Sᴛᴏʀɪᴇꜱ ᴀʙᴏᴜᴛ ᴍʏᴛʜɪᴄᴀʟ ᴄʀᴇᴀᴛᴜʀᴇꜱ are found all over the world. Native Americans say that many monsters peopled the world at the beginning of time, until great heroes defeated them. Some people believe that mythical beasts are based on garbled accounts of real creatures — that unicorns, for instance, are really rhinoceroses. But mythical creatures seem to be more a focus for fear, awe, and wonder than simply mistaken natural history. Monsters are sometimes combinations of various animals, such as the griffin, which was half-eagle, half-lion. Just giving an ordinary animal a special feature, such as the ability of the Greek horse Pegasus to fly, transports it from the ordinary world to a realm of wonder.

WILD HORSES
Half-man, half-horse, the centaur was a wild and savage creature. One exception was Chiron, a wise centaur, who was tutor to many Greek heroes. He died after being accidentally wounded by Heracles with a poisoned arrow.

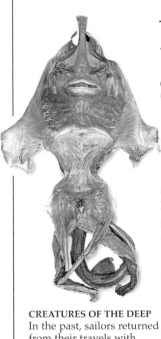

CREATURES OF THE DEEP
In the past, sailors returned from their travels with strange beasts, which they claimed to have fished from the sea. The creature "Jenny Haniver" (above) is actually a dried skate fish. Some of these curious creatures were created by joining the bodies of different animals together. For instance, a monkey's body was grafted onto the tail of a fish to create a merman.

BLOWING HOT AIR
Fire-breathing, winged dragons, who jealously guard their hoards of treasure, feature in many European myths. For instance, the Scandinavian dragon Fafnir was actually a man who turned into a dragon to protect his treasure. Many stories tell of dragon-slaying heroes who rescue maidens or win their hands in marriage. One such hero was Tristan, the Celtic hero who killed a dragon to win the hand of Isolde. Unlike the fearsome European dragon, Chinese dragons are kindly and serpentlike.

Spiky claws protrude from the dragon's wings

Dragons breathe fire through their mouths

HORN OF PURITY
The unicorn was a white horselike creature, with a single spiral horn growing from its forehead. It was said that if a unicorn dipped its horn into water, the water would become pure. In fact, the unicorn was such a powerful symbol of purity that supposed unicorn horns (actually the tusks of narwhal whales) once sold for 20 times their weight in gold; one was even said to be worth a city.

Unicorn horns were prized for their supposed ability to detect poison

DREADFUL LOCKS
Medusa was one of the three Gorgons — hideous creatures with snakes for hair. Anyone who looked at her would be turned to stone. But the Greek hero Perseus killed Medusa by looking at her reflection in a bronze shield as he cut off her head.

Medusa's hair was made of writhing snakes

WINGS OF A HERO
The winged horse Pegasus was ridden by the Greek hero Bellerophon. When his enemies ordered Bellerophon to kill the monstrous Chimera (below), they hoped he would die in the attempt. Instead, however, riding Pegasus, Bellerophon swooped down on the monster from above and riddled it with arrows.

Pegasus was born from Medusa's blood

A serpent formed the Chimera's tail

European dragons have batlike wings

The middle part of the Chimera was a she-goat

HEADS AND TAILS
The Chimera was a fire-breathing monster made up of the body parts of various animals. It was one of the children of the half-nymph, half-serpent Echidna, who also spawned such monsters as the Sphinx and the 100-headed serpent Ladon. The Chimera was slain by the Greek hero Bellerophon.

Thorny hooks protrude from the dragon's tail

The Chimera had the forequarters of a lion

The dragon's skin is covered in scales like those of a serpent or fish

Clawed feet are seen on both Chinese and European dragons

Painting the story

THERE ARE MANY WAYS OF TELLING stories other than through speech, and many myths are "told" through ritual, dance, or art rather than through narrative storytelling. In the chantways (right) of the Native American Navajo, sand painting, song, prayer, dance, and ritual combine to relive complex myths, which are remembered not for their story content but for their healing spiritual power. The Australian Aboriginal stories of the Dreamtime are recalled not just in words and ceremonies but also through traditional designs painted on the body. The same designs are used in bark paintings and the ground paintings of central Australia, which are very similar to Navajo sand paintings.

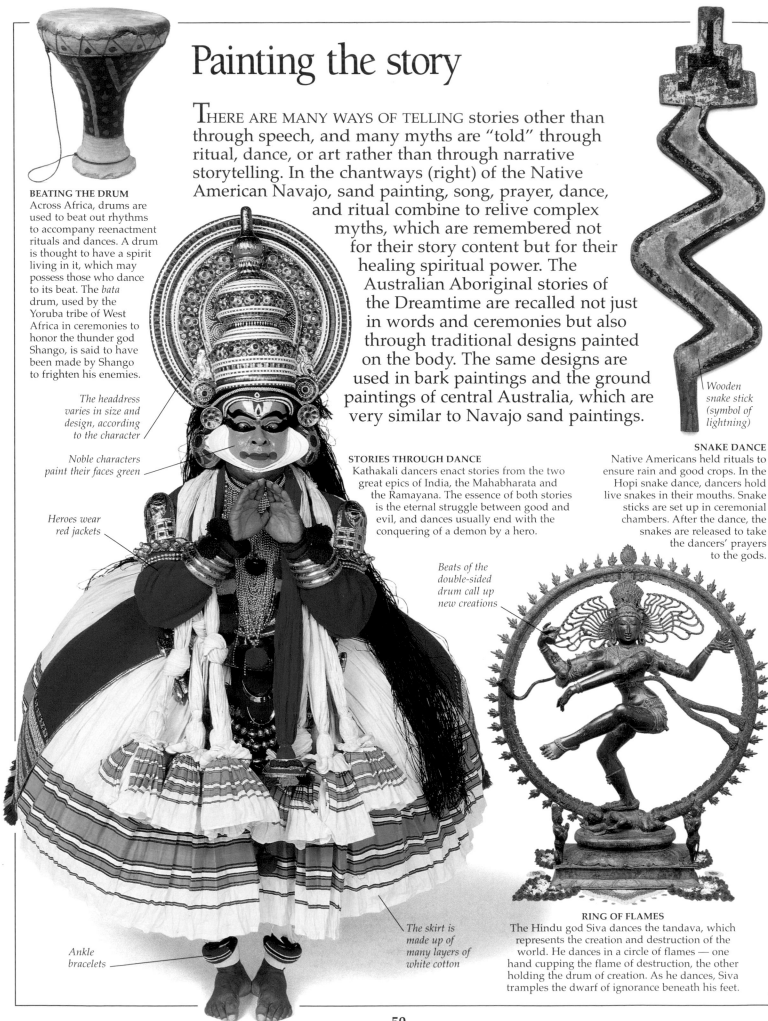

BEATING THE DRUM
Across Africa, drums are used to beat out rhythms to accompany reenactment rituals and dances. A drum is thought to have a spirit living in it, which may possess those who dance to its beat. The *bata* drum, used by the Yoruba tribe of West Africa in ceremonies to honor the thunder god Shango, is said to have been made by Shango to frighten his enemies.

The headdress varies in size and design, according to the character

Noble characters paint their faces green

Heroes wear red jackets

Ankle bracelets

The skirt is made up of many layers of white cotton

Wooden snake stick (symbol of lightning)

SNAKE DANCE
Native Americans held rituals to ensure rain and good crops. In the Hopi snake dance, dancers hold live snakes in their mouths. Snake sticks are set up in ceremonial chambers. After the dance, the snakes are released to take the dancers' prayers to the gods.

STORIES THROUGH DANCE
Kathakali dancers enact stories from the two great epics of India, the Mahabharata and the Ramayana. The essence of both stories is the eternal struggle between good and evil, and dances usually end with the conquering of a demon by a hero.

Beats of the double-sided drum call up new creations

RING OF FLAMES
The Hindu god Siva dances the tandava, which represents the creation and destruction of the world. He dances in a circle of flames — one hand cupping the flame of destruction, the other holding the drum of creation. As he dances, Siva tramples the dwarf of ignorance beneath his feet.

Sacred sandpainting

The sand paintings of the Native American Navajo are temporary altars created and destroyed as part of healing rituals known as chantways. Their Navajo name means "place where the gods come and go." Each painting must be re-created in exactly the same way each time, or the ritual will not work.

Mudstone

Sandstone

Gypsum

Chalk

Brown pigment

Yellow pigment

Red pigment

Charcoal

POWDER PAINTS
Sand painting pigments are gathered by the family sponsoring the ceremony and ground in a mortar and pestle. Pigments include sandstone, mudstone, charcoal from hard oak, cornmeal, powdered flower petals, and plant pollen.

CHANTWAY CEREMONIES
Sand paintings are made by skilled painters under the direction of the singer who is in charge of the ritual. An average sand painting takes six men about four hours to complete. When the painting is finished, the singer sprinkles it with protective pollen and says a prayer; then the ritual begins.

Only men can become qualified sand painters

Pigments are trickled onto the sand through the thumb and forefinger

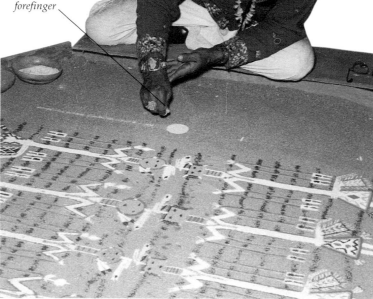

The Oculate Being has bulging eyes

POWERFUL PICTURES
Sand paintings contain exact depictions of the Navajo " holy people" — supernatural beings whose powers are evoked in the chantway ceremonies. Such sand paintings are sacred and powerful. This nonsacred sand painting, made for commercial sale, shows a typical holy person.

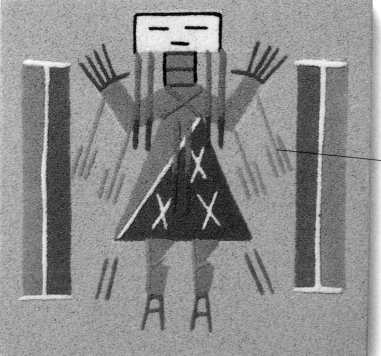

Bracelets and armlets hang from the wrists and elbows

Snake-like tongue

WOVEN STORY
This woven textile from the Paracas people of Peru is full of the spirits and demons of Paracas mythology, including bug-eyed Oculate Beings, shown as heads with no bodies and long tongues snaking out between prominent teeth.

Alpaca wool weaving from southern Peru, 600–200 B.C.

Universal creatures

MANY COMMON THEMES run through world mythology. One theme connects human beings with other animals — we are descended from them, or they are our reincarnated ancestors, or they represent gods or spirits whom we must worship or appease. In many creation myths, such as the stories of the Aboriginal Dreamtime, the first inhabitants of the world are neither animal nor human but a mixture of both. This is true of many "animal" gods, such as the African spider-man Anansi. The Egyptian gods all have one or more animal forms as well as human forms; even in the Judeo-Christian tradition the devil can take the form of a snake.

TURTLE WORLD
Many Native American peoples believe that the Earth is supported on the back of a turtle — a belief that is also found in Hindu mythology. The creator god Brahma took the shape of a turtle to create the world. Vishnu became a turtle to help the gods win the elixir of immortality. In North America and in Africa the turtle is also a trickster figure.

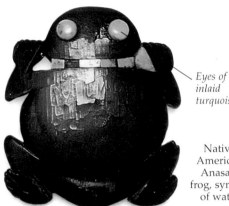

Eyes of inlaid turquoise

Native American Anasazi frog, symbol of water

THE FROG
A West African story telling how Frog brought death into the world is echoed by a Native American myth which says that Frog was so angry with his Maker that he spat poison into the Maker's water, killing him and all his creatures. To the Maori of New Zealand, the frog was a rain god, an association also made by Native Americans. In Egypt Heket was a frog goddess of childbirth and resurrection.

Recurring crocodiles

Because of their fearsome appearance, crocodiles appear in many myths. Often they are threatening creatures — for instance the Basuto tribe of Africa believes that a crocodile can seize a man's shadow and pull him under water. But on the island of Sulawesi, in Indonesia, crocodiles are addressed as "grandfather" because they may be an ancestor. And it is believed that a crocodile will attack a human only when told to do so by the god Poe Mpalaburu.

Detail from a Papuan shield

Man inside the belly of a crocodile

FATHER CROCODILE
Papuans believe that crocodiles have magical powers. One myth of the Kiwai Papuans tells how the creator, Ipila, carved the first four humans from wood and gave them sago to eat. But two of them began to eat meat and turned into crocodile-men. The clans descended from them claim the crocodile as their father.

Turquoise mosaic squares

Coral pieces add color to the nose and mouth

Ceremonial snake pendant worn by priests of the Aztec rain god Tlaloc

LIFE-GIVING SERPENT
The snake is probably the most widely revered creature in world mythology. It is often associated with the primal waters from which all life was created. In the Americas, the double-headed serpent is associated with life-giving rain. Australian Aborigines credit the creation of the landscape to the Rainbow Snake, the source of shamanic power. The Rainbow Snake Aido-Hwedo arches over the sky and under the sea in West Africa.

Egyptian
crocodile god
Sobek

*The crocodile has
large, snapping jaws
with very sharp teeth*

Mayan crocodile
incense burner

HEAVENLY MONSTER
In Mayan art there are numerous depictions of
the celestial, or cosmic, monster, a being with a
crocodile's body and two heads, one at the front
and one at the back. The monster is sometimes
shown arching
over the heavens,
its body in the
form of clouds.

Clawed feet

*Golden crocodile
figure made by the
Ashanti people of
West Africa*

*Dry, scaly skin
prevents water
loss in the hot
African sun*

*Back feet
are webbed*

*Powerful,
whiplike tail*

Nile crocodiles
are found on
riverbanks
throughout
tropical Africa

AFRICAN ANCESTORS
Many Africans believe crocodiles
to be reincarnated people. In West
Africa it is said that a person who
kills a crocodile will become one.
And if someone is attacked by a
crocodile, it is believed that the
victim must have harmed the
crocodile during its human life.

RAVENOUS SOBEK
Ancient Egyptians worshipped
crocodiles in the form of the crocodile
god Sobek, who was often depicted with
the head of a crocodile and the body of a
human. Sobek was so hungry that when the
dismembered body of Osiris was thrown into
the Nile, he ate some of it. The other gods
cut out Sobek's tongue for this wicked act.

Death and the underworld

SINCE HUMANITY BEGAN, PEOPLE HAVE told stories to explain what happens after death. The Mayan hero twins Hunahpu and Xbalanque descended to Xibalba, the "place of fright," to rescue their father from One Death, lord of the underworld. The twins survived ordeals in the houses of lances, fire, and jaguars. They then boasted that they had power over death, and to prove it let themselves be killed and ground like flour. When they came back to life, the lords of death were so impressed that they asked to be killed too. But the twins did not revive them, and so the power of death was lessened forever. In his top hat and dark glasses, the Haitian voodoo god Ghede guards the eternal crossroads where the souls of the dead pass their way to the underworld.

The skeleton is commonly used as an image of death

DYING FOR DISOBEDIENCE
The elaborate funeral rites of the Dogon people of West Africa involve dancing and chanting in a secret language. These rituals recount a myth that describes how death entered the world because of the disobedience of young men. Africans do not see death as a final end but believe that the spirits of the dead have power over the living.

Skirts are red to represent death

CHINESE JUDGE OF THE DEAD
Yen-lo is the terrifying ruler and judge of the dead in China. First, the souls are weighed: the virtuous are light, the sinful heavy. Then the souls must pass a number of tests and challenges. They are assaulted by demons, attacked by dogs, then allowed one last glimpse of home and family before being given a drink that wipes away all memories. Finally, each soul is reincarnated.

Osiris, god of the underworld

Horus, son of Osiris

THE AFTERLIFE
The ancient Egyptians believed that their souls would be weighed against the feather of truth, and that they would then be led into the Hall of the Two Truths to face the lord of the dead, Osiris. The virtuous hoped for a new life in the Field of Reeds, a perfected version of Egypt.

AZTEC LORD OF THE UNDERWORLD

Mictlantecuhtli, the Aztec god of death, is usually depicted as a white skeleton spotted with blood. On their way to his peaceful underworld (Mictlan), the dead were reduced to skeletons by a wind of knives. Mictlantecuhtli was said to be the father of Quetzalcoatl, the lord of life.

The grinning Mictlantecuhtli welcomes the dead to his underworld

DAY OF THE DEAD

The Mexican Day of the Dead (November 1) is an occasion for great festivities. Every family prays to the souls of dead relatives so that they will return to Earth for one night. Altars in homes and cemeteries are decorated with food, flowers, and ghoulish sugar models. A candle is lit for each soul to help it find its way back to the land of the living. Many other cultures celebrate a day of the dead, including the Chinese, where it is known as the Feast of the Hungry Ghosts.

Altar skulls are made from sugar and water and are decorated with sugar icing

Souls of the dead are tormented by demons in hell

VISIONS OF HELL

Eternal torment in the underworld is the fate of sinners in many cultures. The Greeks in particular devised ingenious fates for those who offended the gods. Sisyphus (who told tales on Zeus) was forced to spend eternity rolling a stone uphill, only to see it roll back to the ground just as he was reaching the top. Tantalus (who served the gods his own son at a banquet) was condemned to stand neck-high in water, with ripe fruit dangling over his head, never able to eat or drink.

Norse chieftains were cremated in longboats to transport them to Valhalla

WARRIORS' HEAVEN

Viking warriors longed to be chosen for death in battle by Odin's warrior maidens, the Valkyries. This meant that, instead of going to hell, warriors would experience a glorious afterlife of feasting and fighting in the golden halls of Valhalla. Here they prepare to fight for the gods in the final battle (Ragnarok) of this present world.

White pottery figure of the Aztec lord of death

Sacred sites

T HE ICE AGE CAVE pictures of Europe — and their ancient equivalents in Australia, America, and Africa — show us that humankind has always recognized and respected sacred spaces, where the everyday and the eternal meet. Sacred sites may be temporary or permanent, and the same place may be reused many times. Many Christian churches, for instance, are on the sites of pagan temples. Lakes, rivers, caves, woods, or mountaintops may be as spiritual as a temple or church. A place may declare itself sacred simply by its beauty — something the Japanese recognize in erecting *torii* gates (right), in places that are natural shrines. A totem pole, erected to proclaim a family's mythological descent, is also visible proof that the world of humankind and the world of gods and spirits are one and the same.

Most probably an altar, this flat sandstone block was 16 feet (5 meters) long

STANDING STONES
The building of the great Neolithic temple at Stonehenge in Wiltshire, Great Britain, occurred between about 2500 and 1500 B.C. The sacred stones, which are aligned with the sun, moon, and stars, are thought to have had astronomical connections. Stonehenge was also adopted as a sacred site by the druids, Celtic priests of the Iron Age (c. 1100 B.C.).

Curved ends of horizontal bars reach toward heaven

GATEWAYS TO HEAVEN
A *torii* is a gateless entranceway that marks the point where ordinary space becomes sacred space. A *torii* stands at the entrance to each Japanese Shinto shrine, and also in front of the sacred Mount Fuji (right). Because *torii* means bird, it is sometimes said that the *torii* is erected to provide a resting place for birds, so that their song will please the gods at dawn.

Thunderbird makes lightning by opening and closing its eyes

GREAT PYRAMIDS
The Egyptian sun god Ra was born on a pyramid-shaped piece of land jutting out of the primal ocean. This shape was then adopted by the Egyptian pharaohs (kings) for their tombs, putting them under the protection of the sun god.

The thunderbird creates thunder by flapping its wings

Mythical monuments

The totem poles of North American Indians are carved heraldic monuments displaying images of a family's or clan's mythological descent. Sometimes wealthy families commissioned totem poles as memorials to their dead relatives. The Native American Kwakiutl people say that the first totem pole, *kakaluyuwish* (pole that holds up the sky), was made by Wakiash, a Kwakiutl chief, with knowledge that he won from the animal-people when Raven flew him around the world.

This thunderbird totem pole is among the many historical totem poles that stand in Stanley Park in Vancouver, Canada. *Thunderbird* was copied in 1988 from the original, which was erected in 1927.

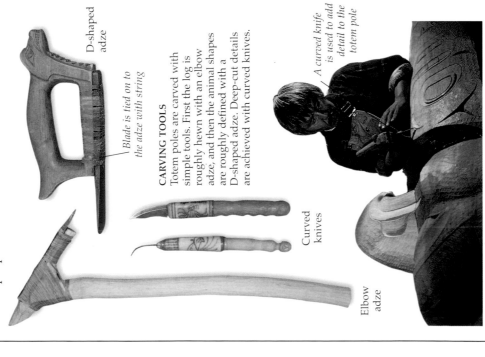

A human ancestor figure

CARVING TOOLS
Totem poles are carved with simple tools. First the log is roughly hewn with an elbow adze, and then the animal shapes are roughly defined with a D-shaped adze. Deep-cut details are achieved with curved knives.

D-shaped adze

Blade is tied on to the adze with string

Curved knives

Elbow adze

A curved knife is used to add detail to the totem pole

WORKING THE WOOD
Totem poles are usually carved from red cedar, which grows up to 200 feet (60 meters) tall. Carvers work up the pole from the bottom to the top, with the pole lying horizontally on its side. The wood is kept soft by dousing it with pans of hot water.

TEMPLE OF THE MAIDEN
The word "parthenon" means "temple of the maiden," and the Parthenon was the great temple of Athena situated on the Acropolis at Athens, in Greece. Athena, goddess of war and wisdom, was the patron of the city. The Parthenon contained her statue in gold and ivory and a frieze depicting battle scenes and processions of worshipers.

GOLDEN WATERS
Gold was so important to the Incas that they called it the sweat of the sun god Inti. At El Dorado lake (above) in Colombia, each new king was coated in gold dust before sailing out to throw gold offerings into the water. The Spanish conquerors of Peru heard rumors of this and searched in vain for the kingdom of El Dorado and its fabulous riches.

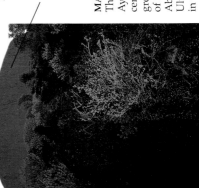

At sunrise and sunset, Uluru displays spectacular shades of orange and purple

MAJESTIC MOUNTAIN
The sacred site of Uluru, or Ayers Rock, rises from the central desert of Australia with great natural majesty. The focus of many myths among the Aborigines of central Australia, Uluru was said to have been built in the Dreamtime by two boys playing with mud after rain.

End of the world

JUST AS MYTHOLOGIES TELL how the world began, so they predict how it will end, often in a terrible fire or flood. The Aborigines of southeastern Australia believed that the end would come when one of the four props that held up the sky rotted away, allowing the sky to fall. The Native American Cherokee believed that the world was a great floating island, held by four cords hanging down from the sky, and that when these rotted through, the Earth would sink back beneath the sea. The ancient Egyptians, who feared every night that the sun god would be defeated in his journey through the underworld and fail to reappear, also foresaw a time when the god would grow so old and tired that he would forget who he was, so that all he had created would come to an end.

The world will end when the rainbow serpent chews his own tail

COSMIC SERPENT
In West Africa Aido-Hwedo, the rainbow snake, carried the creator in his mouth while the world was made, and then circled around the Earth to hold it together. Red monkeys beneath the sea forge iron bars to feed him. When the iron runs out, Aido-Hwedo will chew his own tail, the world will convulse, and the Earth and all its burdens will slide into the sea.

Rocky matter from an explosion in space

The world serpent has many heads

When Brahma awakes, he rises on a lotus flower from the god Vishnu

Lakshmi, Vishnu's wife, the goddess of fortune

At night Vishnu rests on the world serpent, Shesha

END OF THE KALPA
For Hindus, time is an endless cycle of days and nights of Brahma, or kalpas. During the day, when Brahma is awake, the world is created anew; when Brahma goes to sleep, the kalpa ends. Each kalpa lasts 4.32 billion years.

GREAT WORLD POLE

According to the Native American Cheyenne people, the Great White Grandfather Beaver of the North is gnawing the great pole that holds up the world. When he gnaws right through, the world will end. The Tsimshian of the northwest coast say that the pole on which the world spins is held up by Amala. He has a servant who gives him strength by rubbing his back with wild-duck oil once a year. The oil is nearly used up; when it runs out, Amala will die, and the world will fall.

North American family totem (symbol) of the beaver

MYTH OF THE FIVE SUNS

The Aztecs believed that this world was the fifth, and that each creation had its own sun. The fifth sun first shone on August 13, 3114 B.C., and will last until at least A.D. 4772. But it will not last forever, for "all moons, all years, all days, all winds, reach their completion and pass away."

Aztec calendar stone c. 1352

The Sun god Ra in the guise of a cat

Apep, the chaos serpent

EGYPTIAN APEP

Each night, as the sun god Ra voyaged through the underworld, his ship was attacked by the chaos serpent Apep, his mortal enemy. If Apep ever devoured Ra, the world would end. Each night Ra took the form of a cat and cut off Apep's head.

THE BIG CRUNCH

Many mythologies envisage a cycle of creation and destruction and foresee the emergence of a new world after this one ends. According to scientific theory, this is perfectly feasible. The universe, which is currently expanding, may one day reach a maximum size and collapse in on itself in a "Big Crunch." The matter and energy from the collapsed universe may then bounce back to create a new universe.

Midgard serpent — monstrous child of the trickster Loki

LAST BATTLE OF THE NORSE GODS

The warlike Vikings thought the world would end in a final cataclysmic battle, in which all the main gods would die and the Earth would be consumed by fire. This battle is Ragnarok, the twilight of the gods. The wolf Fenrir, child of the trickster Loki, will break his bonds, kill Odin the all-father, and swallow the sun. But from this world's ruin, a new creation will arise.

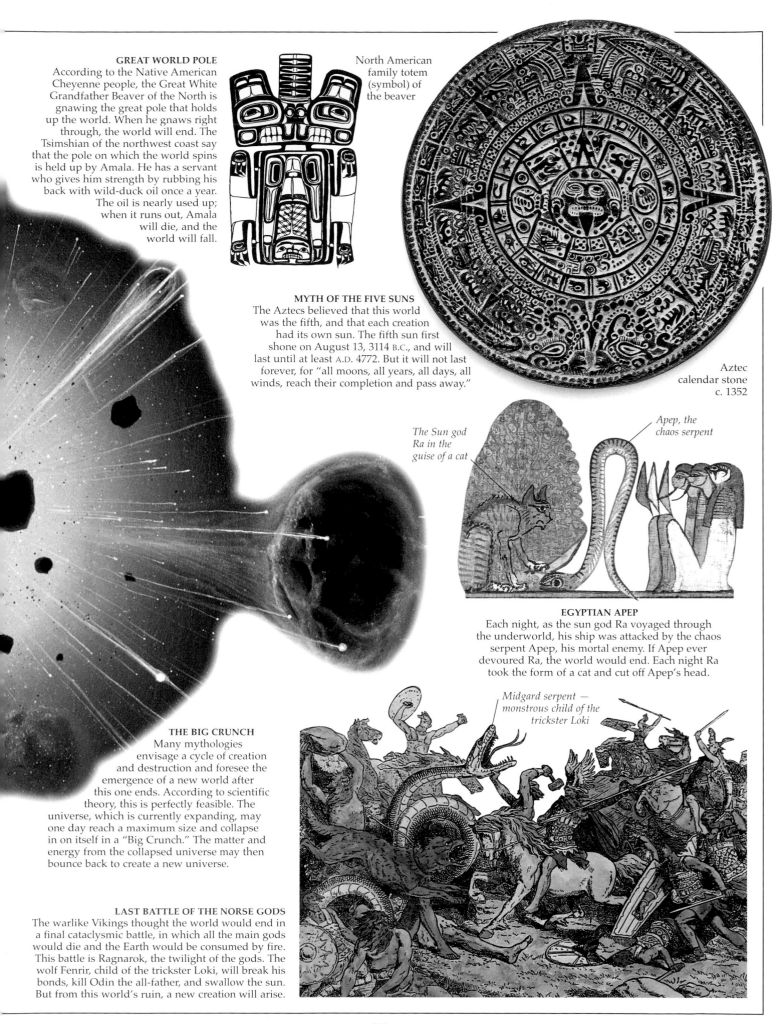

Index

Acknowledgments

Dorling Kindersley would like to thank:
Alan Hills, Philip Nicholls, Christi Graham, John Williams, Kevin Lovelock, Jim Rossiter, and Janet Peckham of the British Museum, London; Kalamandalam Vijayakumar and Kalamandalam Barbara Vijayakumar; and the African Crafts Centre, Covent Garden, London.

Photography: Andy Crawford

Researcher: Robert Graham

Index: Chris Bernstein

Design assistance: Jill Bunyan and Anna Martin

Picture credits
The publisher would like to thank the following for their kind permission to reproduce the photographs:

(t = top, b = bottom, a = above, c = center, l = left, r = right)

AKG London: 39tr, 39l; Boymans van Beuningen Museum, Rotterdam *The Tower of Babel*, Pieter Brueghel the Elder 9r; Erich Lessing /Württembergisches Landesmuseum, Stuttgart 9bcr, 26tl, 46tl; SMPK Kupferstichkabinett, Berlin 14tl; Torquil Cramer 58/59c; Universitets Oldsaksamling, Oslo 34bc; Von der Heydt Museum, Wuppertal Flora, *Awakening Flowers*, 1876, by Arnold Bucklin (1827–1901) 25bl.
American Museum of Natural History: 43br, 50tr, 52cl; Thos. Beiswenger 41r.
Ancient Art & Architecture Collection: D. F. Head 31tr; Ronald Sheridan 10bl, 13br, 23cl, 26br, 27ar, 45l, 45ca.
Ashmolean Museum, Oxford: 16c, 32br, 42/43c.
Duncan Baird Publishers Archive: 16tl; Japanese Gallery 11cr, 33c.
Bildarchiv Preußischer Kulturbesitz: 34tl; SMPK Berlin 18; Staatliche Museum, Berlin 48tr.
Bridgeman Art Library, London/New York: British Museum, London *The Weighing of the Heart Against Maat's Feather of Truth*, Egyptian, early 19th Dynasty, c.1300 B.C., *Book of the Dead of the Royal Scribe* 54br; By Courtesy of the Board of the Trustees of the V & A *Vishnu in the Center of his Ten Avatars*, Jaipur area, 18th century 20tl; Galleria degli Uffizi, Florence, Italy *The Birth of Venus*, c.1485, by Sandro Botticelli (1444/5–1510) 42cl; Louvre, Paris, France/Giraudon *Stele of a Woman before Re-Harakhy*, Egyptian, c.1000BC 15tl; Musée Condé, Chantilly, France MS 860/401 f.7 *The Story of Adam and Eve*, detail from "Cas des Nobles Hommes et Femmes" by Boccaccio, translated by Laurent de Premierfait, French 1465, *Works of Giovanni Boccaccio* (1313–75) 9bl (right), 17br; Museo Correr, Venice, Italy *Glimpse of Hell* (panel) by Flemish School (15th century) 55bl; Piazza della Signoria, Florence/Lauros – Giraudon *Perseus with the Head of a Medusa*, 1545–54, in the Loggia dei Lanzi, by Benvenuto Cellini (1500–71) 35bcr; Private Collection Genesis 6: 11-24 Noah's Ark, Nuremberg Bible (Biblia Sacra Germanaica), 1483 21cb.
British Museum, London: 6br, 6bl, 9bc, 13tr, 14tr, 16r, 17c, 17r, 17r, 18tr, 19r, 23t, 25tl, 28bl, 31br, 35tr, 36c, 38br, 39bc, 42tl, 43tc, 43tr, 52bl, 53tl.
Cambridge Museum of Anthropology: 21r, 57tr.
Central Art Archives: The Old Students House, Helsinki 19tl.
Jean-Loup Charmet: 9tr, 21tl.
Christie's Images: *In the Well of the Great Wave of Kanagawa*, c.1797, by Hokusai Katsushika (1760–1849) 20/21b, 30r, 31l.
Bruce Coleman Ltd: Jeff Foott Productions 44tl.
CM Dixon: 31bc.
Edimedia: 14cr.
E.T. Archive: 33l; British Library Or 13805 56bl; Freer Gallery of Art 24br; Victoria & Albert Museum, London 12/13c.
Mary Evans Picture Library: 12bl, 12br, 23bl, 28c, 30tl, 32bl.
Werner Forman Archive: Anthropology Museum, Veracruz University, Jalapa 55r; Arhus Kunstmuseum, Denmark 32cl; Dallas Museum of Art 28bl; David Bernstein Fine Art, New York 51r; Field Museum of Natural History, Chicago 11t; Museum of the American Indian, Heye Foundation 15cl; Smithsonian Institution 14bl; State Museum of Berlin 18cl.
Glasgow Museums (St. Mungo): 33bl, 34bl, 40bl, 50br, 54tr.
Hamburgisches Museum für Völkerkunde: 45tr.
Robert Harding Picture Library: Patrick Mathews 54bl.
Michael Holford: British Museum 9cr (below), 10bc, 10tl, 15bl, 16bl, 42bl, 57cr; Kunisada 15br; Museum of Mankind 44bl; Victoria & Albert Museum, London 11br.
Hutchison Library: Ian Lloyd 59br.
Images Colour Library: 26c, 57br, 58tr; Impact: Mark Henley 59tr.
INAH: Michael Zabe 21tc, 24l, 18bc.
Barnabas Kindersley: 55tl, 55c (above).
MacQuitty International Photo Collection: 41bl.
The Board of Trustees of the National Museums & Galleries on Merseyside: 30bl, 53tr.
Nilesh Mistry: 32tl.
Musée de L'Homme, France: 22l; D Ponsard 38l, 56tl.
Museum of Anthropology, Vancouver: 59cl.
Museum of Mankind: 6cl, 34c, 37tc.
National Maritime Museum: 4c, 49tr.
National Museum of Copenhagen: 36/37b.
Natural History Museum, London: 4tcl, 29tr, 29c, 48/49b, 48tl, 49tl, 49r.
© David Neel, 1998: 4tl.
Peter Newark's Pictures: 8br, 18r, 41cl, 51c.
Panos Pictures: Caroline Penn 59bl.
Ann & Bury Peerless: 22cl, 47tl.
Pitt Rivers Museum, Oxford: 8bcl, 12tr, 25cr, 40tr 53bl; Zither 19tc.
Planet Earth Pictures: Jan Tove Johansson 10l.
Axel Poignant Archive: 13cl, 23br, 37tl.
Rex Features: Tim Brooke 55bcl.
Rijksmuseum voor Volkenkunde: 22r.
Réunion des Musées Nationaux Agence Photographique: Hervé Lewandowski 28tl, 35cr; Richard Lambert 39cbr.
Science Photo Library: Chris Bjornberg 10/11c; Sally Benusen (1982) 56/57c.
South American Pictures: Tony Morrison 15tr, 59cr.
Spectrum Colour Library: 58cr.
Statens Historika Museum, Stockholm: 9br.
Oliver Strewe: 52cr; 31cra.

Jacket:
American Museum of Natural History: front cl.
Ancient Art & Architecture Collection: front tl, back tl.
Ronald Sheridan inside front cr, back cr.
Ashmolean Museum, Oxford: back bl.
Duncan Baird Publishers Archive: inside front tl.
Bildarchiv Preußischer Kulturbesitz: State Museum, Berlin front c.
British Museum, London: front tc, bc, back tc, bc.
Danish National Museum, Copenhagen: inside front b.
Werner Forman Archive: State Museum, Berlin front tr, back tr.
Hamburgisches Museum für Völkerkunde: inside front cl.
Michael Holford: front tcr, back tcr.
Natural History Museum, London: front r, back cla.
Ann & Bury Peerless: back cra.
Axel Poignant Archive: back br.
Statens Historiska Museum, Stockholm: front tr, back tr.

SUBJECTS

HISTORY

ARMS & ARMOR

BATTLE

CASTLE

COWBOY

EXPLORER

KNIGHT

MEDIEVAL LIFE

MYTHOLOGY

NORTH AMERICAN INDIAN

PIRATE

SHIPWRECK

TITANIC

VIKING

WILD WEST

WORLD WAR I

WORLD WAR II

WITCHES & MAGIC-MAKERS

ANCIENT WORLDS

ANCIENT CHINA

ANCIENT EGYPT

ANCIENT GREECE

ANCIENT ROME

AZTEC, INCA & MAYA

BIBLE LANDS

MUMMY

PYRAMID

THE BEGINNINGS OF LIFE

ARCHEOLOGY

DINOSAUR

EARLY HUMANS

PREHISTORIC LIFE

THE ARTS

BOOK

COSTUME

DANCE

FILM

MUSIC

TECHNOLOGY

BOAT

CAR

FLYING MACHINE

FUTURE

INVENTION

SPACE EXPLORATION

TRAIN

SCIENCE

ASTRONOMY

CHEMISTRY

EARTH

ECOLOGY

ELECTRICITY

ELECTRONICS

ENERGY

EPIDEMIC

EVOLUTION

FORCE & MOTION

HUMAN BODY

LIFE

LIGHT

MATTER

MEDICINE

SKELETON

TECHNOLOGY

TIME & SPACE

SPORT

BASEBALL

OLYMPICS

SOCCER

SPORTS

ANIMALS

AMPHIBIAN

BIRD

BUTTERFLY & MOTH

CAT

DOG

EAGLE &
BIRDS OF PREY

ELEPHANT

FISH

GORILLA,
MONKEY & APE

HORSE

INSECT

MAMMAL

REPTILE

SHARK

WHALE

HABITATS

ARCTIC & ANTARCTIC

DESERT

JUNGLE

OCEAN

POND & RIVER

SEASHORE

THE EARTH

CRYSTAL & GEM

FOSSIL

HURRICANE &
TORNADO

PLANT

ROCKS & MINERALS

SHELL

TREE

VOLCANO &
EARTHQUAKE

WEATHER

THE WORLD AROUND US

BUILDING

CRIME & DETECTION

EVEREST

FARM

FLAG

MEDIA &
COMMUNICATIONS

MONEY

RELIGION

RESCUE

SPY

Future updates and editions will be available online at www.dk.com

DK EYEWITNESS BOOKS

A–Z

Row 1:
DORLING KINDERSLEY EYEWITNESS BOOKS — AMPHIBIAN
DORLING KINDERSLEY EYEWITNESS BOOKS — ANCIENT CHINA
DORLING KINDERSLEY EYEWITNESS BOOKS — ANCIENT EGYPT
DORLING KINDERSLEY EYEWITNESS BOOKS — ANCIENT GREECE
DORLING KINDERSLEY EYEWITNESS BOOKS — ANCIENT ROME
DORLING KINDERSLEY EYEWITNESS BOOKS — ARCHEOLOGY
DORLING KINDERSLEY EYEWITNESS BOOKS — ARCTIC & ANTARCTIC

Row 2:
ARMS & ARMOR · ASTRONOMY · AZTEC, INCA & MAYA · BASEBALL · BATTLE · BIBLE LANDS · BIRD

 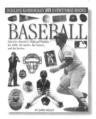    

Row 3:
BOAT · BOOK · BUILDING · BUTTERFLY & MOTH · CAR · CASTLE · CAT

Row 4:
CHEMISTRY · COSTUME · COWBOY · CRIME & DETECTION · CRYSTAL & GEM · DANCE · DESERT

Row 5:
DINOSAUR · DOG · EAGLE & BIRDS OF PREY · EARLY HUMANS · EARTH · ECOLOGY · ELECTRICITY

Row 6:
ELECTRONICS · ELEPHANT · ENERGY · EPIDEMIC · EVEREST · EVOLUTION · EXPLORER

Row 7:
FARM · FILM · FISH · FLAG · FLYING MACHINE · FORCE & MOTION · FOSSIL

Row 8:
FUTURE · GORILLA, MONKEY & APE · HORSE